Culture Starts with You

Leading a Thriving School Community

Bobby Moore, Ed.D.
Foreword by Peter DeWitt, Ed.D.

Association for Middle Level Education
Westerville, Ohio

Printed in the United States of America.

ISBN 978-1-56090-295-9

William D. Waidelich, EdD, CAE—Executive Director
April Tibbles—Chief Communications Officer
Dawn Williams—Publicatons Manager/Designer
Marcia Meade-Hurst— Senior Member Center Specialist

Library of Congress Cataloging in Publication Control Number:
2018022185

Association for Middle Level Education
4151 Executive Parkway, Suite 300
Westerville, Ohio 43081 | amle.org

Contents

"This book caught my attention the same way Dan Goleman did with his original work—an excellent mix of the science, how to apply it, and how to reflect on the way it underpins your own relationships and success. This text really is the best book on emotional intelligence and school leadership available."

– Dr. Ben Palmer,
CEO of Genos International

Dr. Moore shares insightful strategies and mindsets that leaders need to consider in building culture. Through his stories, he provokes reflection for any leader to consider in building a collaborative culture for success. For any leader looking to improve, this book will challenge your thoughts and inspire your heart."

– Neil Gupta, Ed.D.,
District Administrator, Worthington City Schools, Ohio

"Dr. Moore has a clear understanding of what is needed to close the knowing-doing school culture gap. *Culture Begins with You* is a quick and compelling read that packs a powerful punch! Every aspiring and experienced leader will benefit greatly from adding this illuminating resource to his or her learning and leading toolkit."

– Rosa Isiah Perez,
Principal and BAM Radio Network 2016 Thought Leader of the Year

Foreword

In educational leadership, we often hear a lot about change. We hear it so much that we believe our first job is to change things when we get a new leadership position. I believe this feeling that we need to make a change can be destructive. We really need to look for ways to make improvements at the same time we celebrate the success the school community has already achieved.

Where leaders seem to make mistakes is when they chase after improvement without taking into account the human factor, including the culture of the building. It's difficult to make improvements if people in the school community are not aware there is a need to improve. Equally as important is the culture of the school. The culture of the building provides the context for how to move forward.

I received my new position as a principal three months before it officially began. I was still teaching in a neighboring school district, but made the effort to go over to the school that I would lead once a week after school to get to know teachers and meet students when they were there for child care. My predecessor was moving into the role of assistant superintendent, and she allowed me to come over so often because she wanted me to be successful. I took my only two personal days and spent full days at the school before my official starting date of July 1. Although it was stressful to say goodbye to my classroom in one district and get to know people where I would be the principal in another district, it was well worth the time. It provided me with the opportunity to get to understand the culture.

As the former co-chair of the National School Climate Council, I heard people talking about climate and culture, and they seemed to easily interchange the meanings. Climate is how we feel when we walk into a building. What images, books, and curriculum are we confronted with, and do those important elements of school climate represent our diverse school in a positive way? Culture is a bit different. Culture is developed over years and often involves things we do not see. It's less about the curriculum offered—although curriculum is important—and more about who chooses to cover it. Culture is about the ways the curriculum gets taught or whether it gets taught at all.

Climate is what we see when we walk into a building and see images hanging that represent our diverse backgrounds, but culture is what happens to us after we have been there. Culture is complicated because it encompasses all the deeply held views of those within a school, and it includes the way we approach change and improvement. And that is why, if you are interested in improvement, you should read this book.

In the work I do with John Hattie, one of the leading researchers in the world of education, we talk a great deal about school leadership. School leadership overall has a .33 effect size—below the hinge point of .40—which equates to a year's worth of growth for a year's input. One of the reasons why school leadership has a lower effect size is that leaders often chase after the shiny new toy that pops up in a book or on social media. The problem with chasing the toy is that those leaders never take time to understand their current reality and forget to understand the context of their school culture.

On the other side of the complicated coin of school improvement are those leaders who believe they cannot make improvements because the building culture won't support it. Bobby Moore believes different, and he explains why in this book. Moore believes, and rightfully so, that leaders are responsible for improving their school culture before they can make any other improvements in their school.

If we do not change the culture to make it more positive, and focus on lifelong learning, then we will never be able to make sustained, impactful improvements in the school. And since you have chosen the leadership position, the ball is in your court. Improving the culture starts with you.

Peter DeWitt, Ed.D.
Author/Consultant

Preface

This book was developed to support school administrators, teacher leaders, and teachers dealing with the emotions, conflicts, behaviors, and challenges of creating a thriving school culture. A supportive school culture must be built on trust, hope, and respect. When a learning community focuses on the intellectual, emotional, and physical needs of its students, there will be times when the school culture is challenged. For this work is not easy and culture is more than a poster you hang on the wall. Culture is the interactions between colleagues, the words that are spoken, the way we make others feel, and how aligned our behaviors and practices are to the school's values, beliefs, and overall goals. There will be times when we are forced to balance patience and persistence, listen instead of speak, and sacrifice our own needs for the good of the group if we want a great school culture.

From my work with principals and teachers from rural, urban, and suburban districts all over the United States, I have learned that many of the problems in cultivating a thriving school culture are caused by the interactions of the adults, who are in good faith at work on the school's mission. However, as educators (and human beings), our lack of training on team building, collaboration, dealing with change, and leadership creates roadblocks and barriers to success while draining valuable energy, motivation, and enthusiasm. Schools must acknowledge the hard work and behaviors it takes to have a great culture and provide educators with the necessary "non-teaching" skills and organizational capacities. As professionals we need to be able to collaborate, celebrate, dialogue, debate, problem solve, and hold each other accountable so all students learn and remain the main focus of our schools.

This book asks the adults in the school building to question the mindsets, behaviors, and skills that limit them and their schools from becoming all they can be. Schools will become not only places of learning for students and adults, but also places of encouragement, inspiration, and support.

Without question, the challenges of demographics, diversity, and economic disadvantages affect our children. But as school leaders we can cultivate a culture of commitment; lead, collaborate with, and support our staffs as we learn to work together; appreciate each other; and tap into every one of our strengths and abilities. If we do this, I firmly believe we as educators can solve nearly every problem in our schools. Having the ability, knowledge, and skill to work together as adults will help us find the courage to do so.

So, I invite you to use this resource to become a leader who leverages your strengths, refines your weaknesses, and learns new skills to make a difference in your school.

CHAPTER 1
Why Culture Starts with You

"We create our organizational culture by the actions we take."

Jim Whitehurst

Over the past 10 years I have had an opportunity to study, research, and work with some of the highest performing schools across the country. During this time, I was able to coach, network, and learn from some amazing leaders of these highly effective schools. Very often we focused our work and conversations around the characteristics of high performing schools. This approach was utilized so we could develop and articulate simple, yet impactful frameworks by identifying the *Five Strategies for Creating a High-Growth School* (2015, Battelle for Kids).

Interestingly, during my research on high performing schools, I noticed there was always a thriving school culture present; one of trust and respect. These cultures did not confuse cooperation with collaboration. Sometimes there was intense dialogue on what was best for student learning and how to align resources to ensure the school's mission was prioritized. Maintaining a focus on student learning and ensuring there is a thriving school culture is not easy work for any school leader. However, these leaders were fiercely devoted to ensuring that student learning was always the priority and that a healthy school culture was present. In addition, I discovered that there were several common mindsets, dispositions, and practices of the highly effective school leaders leading these schools.

The major limitations to creating the school we want and making the desired level of impact on student learning are the mindsets, dispositions, and emotional intelligence practices of the school's leaders. First let me define how I am using the terms mindsets, dispositions, and emotional intelligence practices. A mindset is a leader's set of assumptions, methods, or notations that the person has and that shape many of his or her beliefs and actions. A disposition is a prevailing tendency or mood. It is an individual's normal behavior, response, and reaction to events. One's disposition may not be his or her "best self" but it is really who that individual is most of the time. Emotional intelligence practices are the behaviors that leaders execute or display, even if those practices stretch the person out of his or her comfort zone and do not come natural to that person.

Mindsets

Over the last decade in education there have been many references to mindsets. Although several mindsets may be beneficial in creating a high performing school and thriving school culture, none may be more important than a mindset of positivity and happiness. But first, let's take a look at a couple other popular mindsets.

All students can learn. This is certainly one of the most important mindsets a school leader can have. Without it, excuses are made, apathy drives the culture, and students lose out. Many people have become familiar with "Growth" vs. "Fixed" mindsets thanks to the work of Carol Dweck. But even before Dweck's work, there were school leaders who came to work every day on a crusade to close equity and opportunity gaps for all children by believing all students can learn and do rigorous work. Those leaders who have a mindset that all students can learn are relentless in finding ways to connect, support, and reach all students.

Teacher collaboration over isolation. School leaders must stop allowing teachers to work in isolation. The smartest person in the room is always the room. The leaders who have developed the mindset that only through teacher collaboration will the school improve, easily make decisions on how they leverage their time, talent, and resources. There are enough case studies and research that show investing in social capital (teamwork and collaboration) will move a school forward faster and farther than focusing on individual teacher quality.

Happiness and optimism. Teachers and school leaders can cultivate the mindset that has been empirically proven to fuel greater success and fulfillment. The old paradigm, "If I am good at my job, my students learn at high levels, and if I am highly successful, it will bring me happiness," has now been debunked by more than a decade of groundbreaking research in the fields of positive psychology and neuroscience. Applying the research of positive psychology in our schools is more than telling staff to be happy, to focus on the positive aspects of their jobs, and pretend challenges and obstacles do not exist. To embed these practices, we must change our mindsets that have had a negative impact on success and fulfillment. As Shawn Achor, author of *The Happiness Advantage: The Seven Principles of Positive Psychology that Fuel Success and Performance at Work* explains, "Happiness is not the belief that we don't need to change. It is the realization that we can. Happiness and optimism are the precursors to success, not merely the result."

Dispositions

Dispositions are deep in our DNA. Although some dispositions can help us be more successful, there are other dispositions (impulsive, not empathetic, argumentative) that can have a negative impact on leadership and relationships. Learning how to leverage your positive dispositions and the skills to mitigate your negative dispositions are skills that great leaders have. With enough practice and coaching, positive dispositions can be developed or refined.

Emotional Intelligence Practices

While there is certainly a prerequisite of having strong interpersonal skills, constructive mindsets, and positive dispositions to be a successful school leader, these attributes by themselves are not enough. Many education researchers and coaches talk about mindsets, disposition, and skill and knowledge. However, we know from years of research that there is a huge knowing and doing gap, and those with skills are not always disciplined enough to use their skills on a regular and consistent basis. So, I like to refer to actual behaviors and practices. Leaders need to be effective at modeling or demonstrating appropriate behaviors and practices.

Moving Forward

The role of school leader is more challenging than ever. As we strive to promote equity and opportunity for all children, there will always be challenges and possible setbacks. However, school leaders can thrive in this environment with the right mindsets, dispositions, and emotional intelligence practices. While you may or may not possess all or any of these attributes, they can be developed through coaching and feedback. The most common mindsets, dispositions, and practices associated with the most effective leaders are closely aligned with a person having high levels of emotional intelligence. This is why the focus of this book is emotional intelligence and its impact on school culture.

The last several years have been challenging for educators as a plethora of policies, initiatives, and school reform efforts, even though they may have been introduced with good intentions, have challenged schools to maintain a positive and thriving school culture. Whether it's been new evaluation systems, growth measures, new standards, new assessments, Race to the Top or the Every Student Succeeds Act (ESSA), school cultures have suffered, and many have become toxic.

Who is to blame for the eroding school cultures across the country? All of us! We are all responsible for our own happiness, our relationships with each other, and the behaviors we exhibit that have a direct impact on the culture in our schools. However, no one is more responsible than the school principal. In a 2017 report from CultureIQ, "Key Lessons from Top Cultures for 2017," leadership was identified as the key differentiator in culture. School leadership matters more now than ever.

Establishing a healthy school culture is just one of the many skills required for successful school leadership in the 21st century. The CultureIQ report identified (1) Work Environment, (2) Support, and (3) Mission and Value Alignment as "what matters most" in high performing cultures. The late Rick DuFour, the godfather of professional learning communities, stated we should compare our cultures to gardens and consider our school leaders the gardeners. Highly effective gardeners know how to fertilize the soil, water regularly, and even when to pull toxic weeds. The experienced gardener is not surprised how long it takes to nurture and cultivate a thriving garden.

Modeling the work of a gardener in your school may not be difficult or highly strategic work, but nonetheless, it needs to be prioritized and demonstrated regularly. That is why we will use the word *cultivate* in association with culture rather than *build*. We do not want to assume you can build a school culture and walk away, and it will care for itself. It needs constant attention and care. To cultivate a culture that is collaborative, focused, always challenging the status quo, where excellence is the expectation, and strong relationships and trust thrive, one will need to (1) take responsibility for one's own happiness and fulfillment, (2) develop and demonstrate behaviors—including high levels of emotional intelligence—that motivate (not de-motivate) and encourage your staff, and (3) learn specific skills, strategies, and practices that can improve organizational health and school culture.

Reflection

People who are successful in their lives personally and professionally usually take time to reflect. Highly effective leaders are no different. At the end of each chapter there will be prompts that will allow you to reflect. To maximize the benefit of your learning, please take time to do so. You will also find that regular reflection at the end of the day and week will be one of the strategies recommended for honing your own leadership skills. The importance of regularly reflecting on your dispositions and moods, behaviors, emotions, decisions, and interactions with others is key to becoming a highly effective leader. Some even share their reflections with trusted colleagues or seek feedback while replaying their interactions with others.

Why School Culture?

In my first book, *Inspire, Motivate, Collaborate,* I wrote "Future school leaders will need to transform schools into autonomous, systems-thinking organizations based on professional learning communities that embrace change and create high performing learning environments for students and teachers" (Moore, 2007). Ten years later, I have evolved my view to, "Future school leaders will need to transform schools into autonomous, systems-thinking organizations that simultaneously focus on deep implementation of high impact strategies and cultivate a culture built on trust, collaboration, and respect." Culture trumps strategy, and great school culture eats strategy for breakfast every single day! For years schools have focused on pedagogy, leadership, school schedules, and other strategies strongly believed to be associated with student learning. We know now that cultivating a culture of trust, engagement, collaboration, and morale is equally important. In *Good to Great* (Collins, 2001), great organizations moved away from the "tyranny" of *or* and embraced the "genius" of *and*. It's time for schools to do the same and realize a thriving and healthy school culture is as important as the high leverage strategies employed in the classrooms and building. It is my goal that this book and the strategies within will help you be a better leader and assist you in cultivating a positive, thriving culture.

CHAPTER 2
Mindsets

"Success is not the key to happiness. Happiness is the key to success. If you love what you are doing, you will be successful."

Herman Cain

Thomas has always been an enthusiastic, empathetic, skillful, and happy school teacher and principal. He recently finished his tenth year in education, his third year as a middle school principal, and he celebrated his 35th birthday. Thomas is also married and has two small children, both of whom are too young to start school. His wife Jessica was a university professor, and they both enjoyed their careers in education.

In his early years, Thomas was an excellent middle school math teacher and track coach. He understood pedagogy and was a master in formative assessment practices. His relationships with students, staff, and administration were second to none. He even had great relationships with nearly every parent in the community. Every year his students' math scores ranked among the best in the state, and his track team competed for league championships. When a middle school principal's job became available in a neighboring district, Thomas could not contain himself from the opportunity to lead a building, although he knew he would be leaving a wonderful staff, talented leaders, and trusting relationships he had spent years developing.

Thomas's first couple years as a rookie principal at Brookhaven Middle School were amazing. His reputation as an excellent teacher, trusting colleague, and empathetic leader followed him and allowed him to develop strong relationships with his new community, students, teachers, and administration. The school's academic program quickly turned around, and the school's ranking in the state improved each of the last three years. Most recently, they were in the top 10% in the state. Thomas's focus on collaboration, teamwork, and empowerment not only resonated with the teaching staff, but inspired them to new heights. Brookhaven's school culture had to be among the best in the country! Much of it had to do with Thomas's leadership style and how much he loved his job. It brought joy to his life working with students and teachers.

However, during the summer between his third and fourth year, the unimaginable happened. Thomas's wife announced to him that she had accepted a new position as a professor across the country and wanted a divorce. Thomas was devastated and never saw this coming as he believed everything was bliss and happiness in his marriage. Yes, they both worked a lot of hours, yet they spent quality time together with their children. The only acceptable news of this announcement was that Jessica shared she did not want to take the children with her. She felt she could not establish a new career and be successful with all the new responsibilities of teaching and publishing that came with her new appointment. In what seemed more like hours than months, the summer was over, Jessica had moved across the country, and school was starting back.

Thomas's fourth year at Brookhaven did not resemble his first three years. Even though Thomas was lucky to have family in the area and childcare was not a problem, Thomas could not move on from what he described as the most devastating event in his life. Thomas seemed to no longer experience joy in his life, despite having two beautiful children and a position in a school where he was respected and experienced a great deal of success. During the year, he was short with parents, at times disrespected his faculty members, and was not nearly as engaged with the students as he was previously. On several occasions during the year, the school superintendent Dr. Williams and a fellow principal (Mike Green) who was his friend tried to intervene. However, little progress was shown; in fact things seemed to get worse. Before spring break, Dr. Williams called Thomas into his office with great concern. He shared with Thomas that he had tried to be patient and understanding with him. However, he had seen very little progress with his moods and behavior towards others. Dr. Williams mentioned that Thomas had staff members who had divorced, lost a child to cancer, and experienced other tragedies in their lives, but they all seemed to have managed to not let personal events distract them from healthy relationships and their responsibilities. Dr. Williams suggested that Thomas consider getting counseling and perhaps take spring break to focus on a strategy for improvement. Dr. Williams also informed Thomas that if his behaviors continued, he would have no other choice than to non-renew his contract as he must focus on the culture of the school. Even though Thomas took his advice and started to see a counselor, there was little improvement in Thomas's behaviors and his tenure at Brookhaven came to an end in June. Now Thomas was not only single, but unemployed.

A New Beginning

June ended with much sadness for Thomas. How was he going to support two children and get his life back? Would he find a new job? Then in July his phone rang, and it was his colleague, Mike Green, who was no longer a principal but an assistant superintendent in the Western Hills School District. Western Hills just lost one of their middle school principals to retirement and Mike thought Thomas could be the right person for the job. Western Hills is a much more challenging district and did not have the wealth of Thomas' previous district, but as Mike put it, "lots of potential." Mike said he shared with the superintendent about the success that Thomas experienced during his first three years at Brookhaven Middle School and the challenges Thomas experienced last year. Mike said the interviews would occur in about three weeks and asked Thomas to consider applying for the job. Thomas said he would and felt that this could be his second chance.

Thomas went to the bookstore and looked for some books on changing behaviors and choices. He noticed many of them had a theme around mindsets and dispositions. Thomas was attracted to one specific book written by a Harvard professor on happiness. Thomas took the books with him to the next counseling session. His counselor shared that yes, indeed, there is a great deal of research around how one's mindset can help people overcome challenges, obstacles, and setbacks. Thomas was excited to learn more.

Three weeks flew by and Thomas interviewed with the superintendent and an interview team of staff and parents. Thomas was not sure if anyone really knew about his last year at Brookhaven, but in the interview the subject came up. Thomas focused on his first three years at Brookhaven and shared briefly how a personal setback prevented him from being as effective as he could. He even shared how his colleagues tried to help and how he put the blame on only himself. Thomas stated that serving students and staff was his calling and believed that the past experience would make him even more grateful and more effective in another position. Thomas got the job.

The first day of school was Thomas's most challenging day ever. He had to deal with a student discipline issue on the bus, a frustrated staff member who was reassigned to his building, and an angry parent who was upset about the increased cost of school supplies. Thomas enjoyed every bit of it. This is what he was born to do.

Positive School Culture

We all have challenges, obstacles, and setbacks in our lives. Some people are more resilient than others. Some bounce back quicker than others. Some just never miss a beat and continue to be positive, focused, and engaged. Unhappy principals cannot lead a positive culture. Your mindset (and dispositions) will have a direct impact on your school. If you show up to work with anxiety, depression, anger, or resentment, I can assure you that your school culture will be no different. There is a science called positive psychology that studies the impact and results of maintaining a positive attitude and happiness and being thankful for the positive aspects of your life.

When I first heard Shawn Achor's TED talk, I did not immediately make the connection to how his research could improve schools. I viewed it as an opportunity to work on my own mindset and behaviors, which hopefully would contribute to my own success and fulfillment. That changed after I saw Shawn's keynote at an education conference, during which he talked about the transformation of Cardinal School District in Iowa. The new superintendent of Cardinal, Joel Pederson, turned around the culture and performance of the district by implementing Achor's core principles from *The Happiness Advantage*. After reading Achor's book, I realized that each of us is responsible for our own happiness and that we have the formula for success backwards. It used to be believed that if you work hard and stay focused, happiness will follow. The truth is if you focus on maintaining a positive outlook and focus on your own happiness, success will follow! And research now proves this!

Positive psychology is not about faking emotions around an unrealistic view of the world, your obstacles, and your surroundings. What positive psychology is suggesting is that if you take the necessary steps to be positive, show gratitude, and reflect on the good things that are happening, your life will be more fulfilled, you will be happier, and success will follow.

I was excited about the potential of Achor's research to help create more positive school cultures, but I was still a little skeptical about how. So, I reached out to Dr. Randy Poe, a former Kentucky Association of School Administrators and Kentucky School Boards Association Superintendent of the Year, who had also brought *The Happiness Advantage* to Boone County Schools. Over the years, I have come to respect Randy as a leader committed to pedagogy and research. His district is one of the highest performing in the state of Kentucky, and I frequently bump into him and his staff at national conferences sharing the district's work.

I asked Randy bluntly, "Why did you choose to implement Shawn Achor's work in Boone County? Is it really needed, or did it turn out to be a distraction to all the other great things you are doing?" He paused for a second to reflect and then said confidently, "Jim Collins (*Good to Great*, 2001) discussed the importance of getting the right people on the bus, Daniel Pink (*Drive*, 2009) shared how to keep those people engaged and motivated, and Shawn Achor's work is important because it not only keeps the wheels on the bus, but keeps them moving in the same direction. Culture matters!" Randy is so committed to the power of positive psychology in schools that he requires all new leaders to develop a 21-day action plan on how they will develop their own mindsets and behaviors (one of Achor's principles). He also clearly communicates to principals that they are responsible for their school's culture (and results). This conversation confirmed for me the importance of working with leaders and teachers and giving them the tools and resources to own their own happiness.

Tools for Developing a Positive Mindset

There are specific, research-proven strategies for developing and maintaining a positive mindset. If applied regularly, personal satisfaction, fulfillment, and performance will increase.

Attitude for gratitude. Taking the time to demonstrate gratitude and appreciation for others is a powerful strategy for increasing one's happiness. Before reading another word, stop what you are doing and identify three contacts in your cell phone that you have not spoken to in a while. Send each person a text and let them know how much you value their friendship, appreciated something kind they did for you, or how much you think of them as a person. Keep the text short, it does not have to be a novel. Wait for about 30 minutes and check your phone. Did you get a response? I'm sure you did. How did that make you feel? We do not show gratitude because we expect something in return. We show gratitude to create positive events in other people's lives. However, there is always a return on investment. When you take the time to show and demonstrate gratitude, some always seem to come back.

Random acts of kindness. One of my good friends is a former Mississippi superintendent of the year. He and his wife are two of the kindest souls I have ever met. One time while visiting his home we came across a homeless man. My friend immediately reached in his car and pulled out what he called a "blessing bag." In the blessing bag was a bottled water, snacks, gum, a gift card to a restaurant, and toiletries. The homeless man was so appreciative. My friend says he and his wife always carry blessing bags with them just to let those who may be down on their luck know that someone cares about them. When I returned home I could not wait to make blessing bags. My wife and I shopped and purchased gallon size plastic bags and filled them with gloves, water, snacks, food, gum, toothbrush and toothpaste, a gift card to a restaurant, wet wipes, and a note of hope for that person. I even took my blessing bag to work and posted a Blessing Challenge on Facebook to encourage others to do the same. I was amazed at how many people shared with me that their children started to do this, or it was being done at their churches and workplaces.

A random act of kindness does not have to be a gift or something that requires financial investment. It can be as little as opening the door, helping people carry something on the street, or even positive notes that you write. The important thing here is to do it. When you do something kind for someone, it makes you feel better about yourself.

Journaling. Do you want to double the positive effect that showing gratitude or doing a random act of kindness has on you? Write about it! Research shows that journaling about positive things you have done or experienced and the emotions you experienced while doing them will have twice the impact on your happiness and fulfillment. It's like you get to relive the experience.

Fun fifteen. We all know the research behind the benefits of regular exercise. Unfortunately, we sometimes put off our exercise because of time constraints and other commitments. While there may be debate on how much a person has to train or run to get the real benefits of strength development or cardiovascular health, just 15 minutes of exercise per day can contribute to better fulfillment and happiness.

Summary

There are no great cultures led by unhappy and disengaged leaders. There is the 20 square feet rule that implies you must take care of everything within your own 20 square feet before you can have any impact on others or school culture.

Reflection

1. Have you ever allowed a personal or professional setback to affect your performance in your job? How did you recover?

2. What strategies work best for you for staying positive and engaged?

3. Choose one of the four strategies for improving your own happiness and do them for a week. During the week, do a journal about them for a doubling effect. What difference in your life did this make?

CHAPTER 3
Dispositions

"I am determined to be cheerful and happy in whatever situation I may find myself. For I have learned that the greater part of our misery or unhappiness is determined not by our circumstance but by our disposition."

Martha Washington

Dispositions

Dispositions are deep in our DNA. Although some dispositions can help you be more successful, there are other dispositions (impulsive, not empathetic, argumentative) that can have a negative impact on your leadership and relationships. Learning how to leverage your positive dispositions and the ability to mitigate your negative dispositions are skills that great leaders have. With enough practice and coaching, positive dispositions can be developed or refined. Here are five of the dispositions found in many successful school leaders.

Confident. One of the most common dispositions is that highly effective principals are confident. Many work hard to balance their egos with humility. Jim Collins described the most effective leaders as "Level 5 Leaders," stating that they are ambitious for the success of their organization or their cause. Level 5 school leaders are focused on making decisions based on what is best for student learning and ensuring equity within their school. Successful school leaders are not afraid to make decisions on what is best for student learning, even if they are often second guessed or criticized like so many of our leaders. One prominent leader stated, "We live in a society obsessed with public opinion, but leadership has never been about being popular." Highly effective principals have the confidence to lead despite their critics.

The challenge for most new school leaders is usually not confidence in themselves, but confidence to take action. There are examples of schools all over the country in which special education students are still removed from the classroom, barriers and obstacles discourage minority students from advanced and rigorous courses, ineffective teachers remain in the classroom, and school schedules continue to be built around beans, balls, and busses instead of student learning as the focal point. To address such issues not only requires a leader with confidence in him or herself, but one with confidence to advance the moral imperative of keeping student learning as the focus of the school. The first step for confident leaders is to move schools from a focus on teaching to a focus on student learning.

Just this past year I engaged in a conversation with a school board member and a central office administrator from an affluent, yet under-achieving school district. The district does well when you control for poverty and exclude minority students from the data; however, that population is growing and the district has quickly become one of the most underperforming districts in their state. The board member and central office administrator (and even the school leaders) in that district are very confident leaders in their own right. People lacking in confidence usually do not run for school board seats or make the move to the central office to take on more responsibility. However, when left to make important decisions that are best practices and ensure equity across the district, few of the leaders were willing to upset the apple cart unless they could get all of the teachers and members of the union on board. This is when we need more confident school leaders more than ever before. When we put job security, unions, and other people's fear ahead of what is best for student learning, then schools will always be stuck, and our students may never get an opportunity to reach their fullest potential. As Rick DuFour once said, "if we wait for everyone to get on the school improvement train, that baby ain't ever going to leave the station."

There are also examples of confident school leaders who moved too fast with a school initiative. There is an old African phrase that says, "if you want to go fast, go alone. If you want to go far, go together." The real challenge for confident school leaders is to balance "loose-tight leadership," autonomy and structure, staff relationships and student outcomes, and doing what is comfortable for others instead of what is best for student learning. There will always be competing values in every organization. Is there strategy for getting more staff members to take ownership? I choose not to use the word "buy-in" which can mean you are selling something. Is there an opportunity to take a coalition of the willing and move forward and bring others along? Whatever the strategy for moving forward, it takes a truly confident leader to focus on the moral imperative and prioritize student learning.

Risk taker and decisive. Recently Forbes listed "decisiveness" as one of the most important characteristics of successful CEOs. Highly effective school leaders are not afraid to make decisions and take risks. In this era of "risk management," and of schools suffering from "paralysis by analysis," highly effective leaders learn by doing and are action oriented. This does not mean they are careless or make decisions haphazardly, but it means they operate from a "Ready, Fire, Aim" perspective. Those who always operate from a "Ready, Aim, Fire" modality usually do not have the confidence to take risks. Great schools have teachers and leaders who learn by doing and are not afraid of failure.

Most people live in their comfort zone, but it's only when we get out of our comfort zone into the risk zone when learning takes place. The risk zone (clearly also the learning zone) is where we are challenged, stimulated, and more importantly, where we grow. As leaders, we need to nudge people out of their comfort zones. You show me a school where the adults are not learning, and I will show you a school where the students are not learning. The challenge is what I mentioned earlier about confidence. If we go too fast without any support, our staff will move into the danger zone. It's within this zone where people get frustrated and disengaged. Great leaders know how to keep their hand on the thermostat and turn the temperature up to move people out of the comfort zone and turn the temperature back to keep people out of the danger zone.

One of the most important practices, which we'll discuss later in the book in more detail, is collecting sources of information while taking a risk. There are times when a leader may slow down, speed up, do some course corrections, pause completely, and even abandon the action when taking risks. This can only happen when the school leader is open to feedback and input before and during implementation.

Empathetically assertive. Being empathetic and assertive are certainly competing values. However, highly effective principals know how to balance patience and persistence. They know how to view things from the perspective of others and understand the human challenges associated with change. While understanding the challenges, highly effective leaders are not afraid to move forward, even with only a few early adopters. People resisting change wait for positive leaders to become frustrated, exhausted, and give up. While leading change, these principals praise and recognize those moving forward and continue to coach those reluctant to change by building relationships and being empathetic. The leaders who do not display empathy for those that are asked to change behaviors and attitudes can sabotage their own efforts.

During all my years researching high performing schools and effective leaders, this may be one of the most prevalent dispositions among the high flyers. People need to know you care about them as a person when nudging them out of their comfort zone. People must know the leader is empathetic and will always be approachable to hear concerns. The most highly effective principals are empathetically assertive when leading their schools. This disposition is associated with emotional intelligence

Learner. To effectively lead a learning organization, a school leader must be a learner. In fact, I often state that it is more important to be a "learning leader" rather than an "instructional leader." Highly effective school leaders keep current in the field by reading journals and books, being active in their professional organizations, and going to conferences and workshops. They observe data from other high performing schools and are always exploring strategies to help their school get better. But the learning does not stop there. These leaders share and practice what they learn. These leaders know the real learning happens when knowledge is put into practice.

School leaders should invest 3% of their time and salary into their professional growth. If a school principal is working 60 hours per week and making $100,000 per year, he or she should be learning 1.8 hours per week (reading, taking a class, collaborating with others) and investing $3000 in professional development (books, conferences, courses, etc.) A school that has leaders and teachers who are growing will have students who are growing.

Sense of humor. Great leaders never take themselves too seriously. They like to laugh and have fun and love to see others having fun. Sense of humor is certainly one characteristic that stands out among many highly effective leaders. If you are going to lead a school by working with teachers and students and partnering with parents, a great sense of humor is advantageous. You can ease tensions, deescalate conflict, increase positive interactions with others, and reduce stress. Having a sense of humor allows leaders to make a positive impact on others as well as themselves. There is a difference between having a sense of humor and just being funny. A sense of humor is an attitude you adopt where you find humor in even the most challenging circumstances instead of getting upset about everything.

Reflection

1. What dispositions do you feel are your strengths and how do you leverage them to improve your school?

2. What dispositions are sometimes a barrier for you to reach your intended outcomes?

3. Describe a time when you demonstrated empathy for an underperforming staff member, yet was clear on the next steps needed for improvement.

Steps to Improve Your Disposition

1. Identify your three most positive dispositions. Over the next month keep a journal and log how you used those dispositions to improve relationships with staff, students, or parents.

2. Keep a journal of any negative interactions or experiences you have at school for one month. Each week reflect on the events that led to the interactions or experiences. Reflect to explore if any of your dispositions were a root cause. If so, how might you prevent a similar interaction or experience from happening in the future?

3. In a journal, identify times during the month in which you could have demonstrated more confidence or taken a risk. If doing so, would the outcome have been different? How might you encourage yourself in the future to be more confident or take a risk?

CHAPTER 4
Emotional Intelligence

"When dealing with people, remember you are not dealing with creatures of logic, but with creatures of emotion."

Dale Carnegie

The Need for Emotional Intelligence

As schools struggle to balance autonomy and mandates, collaboration and teamwork, and patience and persistence, school administrators are expected to be more skilled than at any other time in the history of education. There is sufficient evidence that leaders high in emotional intelligence are more effective and demonstrate more transformational leadership behaviors (Barling, Slater, & Kelloway, 2000; George, 2000; Law, Song, & Wong, 2004). Learning to deal with the emotions of all stakeholders including parents, students, and staff, and learning to recognize and manage your own emotions are challenging tasks. However, research has indicated that emotional intelligence can be developed and improved (Sala, 2001).

Successful reform efforts empower teachers to become active participants rather than just spectators (Ashton & Webb, 1986), but many principals do not have the skills required to support, coach, and listen, and to balance patience and persistence during such a transformation (Moore, 2007).

Sarason (as cited in DuFour & Eaker, 1998) stated that "the turmoil associated with school reform cannot be avoided, and how well it is coped with separates the boys from the men and the girls from the women" (p. 49). Without leaders who understand, accept, and work with the emotions associated with school reform, the intellectual, collaborative, and social capacities of students and teachers may never reach their full capacities. Many students and teachers will forever be limited by the current archaic educational systems in which they function. Those most successful in leading reform are usually referred to as change agents and are not "particularly popular" (Reeves, 2002, p. 41). Sometimes it is not enough to rely on persuasion, collaboration, and inspiration to lead school reform, so leaders will have to be "empathetically assertive" when needed (Goleman, 1995). Such leaders are usually highly skilled in dealing with their emotions as well as the emotions of others.

Emotional Intelligence and School Leadership

In one of the largest studies on emotional intelligence and school leadership, Stone, Parker, and Wood (2005) studied 464 principals or vice principals (187 men and 277 women) from nine different public school boards in Ontario, Canada. Researchers discovered principals and vice principals in the above-average leadership group scored higher than the below-average leadership group on total emotional intelligence in an assessment measuring four broad dimensions (intrapersonal, interpersonal, adaptability, and stress management). The above-average leadership group also scored higher than the below-average leadership group in behavior- and task-oriented skills of empathy and interpersonal relationships, but not of social responsibility. Concluding by advocating that professional development include programs on empathy, emotional self-awareness, and flexibility, the authors proposed using emotional intelligence assessment in recruiting school leaders.

Developing emotional intelligence in school leaders is critical to meeting the needs of a staff that is engaged in developing a common vision for their school, maintaining a focus on high achievement for all students, and creating a school culture of trust and respect. An overwhelming body of research is clear that school culture and ethos can increase engagement, productivity, and accelerate student learning. Great school leadership and positive school culture matter. One is not more important than the other, nor can either exist independent of the other.

Over the past decade, we have called for principals to be instructional leaders, lead learners, learning leaders, managers, data gurus, and hiring experts, among many other duties. However, the field of education has been slow to recognize the importance of emotional intelligence as a key skill for principal success. Michael Fullan, one of the leading authorities on educational leadership, has indicated that the future of the school administrator in the 21st century appears to be tied more closely than ever to establishing successful and harmonious relationships. Well, the future is now! We can no longer ignore the importance of emotional intelligence for school leaders and the impact that leadership has on school culture.

Emotional intelligence, or EI, can be defined as an "ability to monitor one's own and others' feelings and emotions, to discriminate among them, and to use this information to guide one's thinking and action" (Salovey & Mayer, 1990, p.189). Fullan (2001, p.74) stated, "In a culture of change, emotions frequently run high," and added that emotional intelligence, creating successful relationships, and leading change will be the responsibility of all future principals.

Emotional intelligence is a critical skill for school administrators to build trust, increase staff engagement, and create a culture where teaching and learning thrive. For leaders to navigate the complex environment of education today, they need feedback and support to improve their skills as instructional and learning leaders, strong collaborators, and effective communicators, and they need to deal with the emotions of others as well as their own.

While there are as many emotional intelligence frameworks as the number of emotions a student or teacher experiences during a typical school year, we will focus on the six core skills of emotional intelligence from Genos International (2005), and cover each of them in the following chapters.

1. **Self-Awareness:** What limits our ability to overcome challenges? Deal with change? Manage conflict? Reduce stress? Improve our leadership effectiveness? The answer is our self-awareness, or the skill of perceiving and understanding one's own behaviors and emotions. Our

emotions drive our behaviors. Leaders' behaviors influence culture, which impacts results and the performance of others.

2. **Awareness of Others:** How do leaders know when to slow down or speed up when implementing change? How do they understand different working styles, when to dig deeper for more feedback, or how to explore what people are thinking and feeling? Those who have a skill in perceiving other emotions can navigate the challenges associated with school improvement. These leaders are usually skilled at listening, affirming people's thoughts and feelings, and helping them feel valued.

3. **Authenticity:** Despite good intentions, some leaders may seem guarded, blunt, or appear that they will do anything to avoid conflict. This can lead to a culture of mistrust and artificial harmony. Leaders skilled in emotional expression are effective at giving feedback, fostering trust, and expressing their thoughts, opinions, and feelings at the right time and in the right way.

4. **Emotional Reasoning:** Leaders skilled in emotional reasoning have a talent for not only analyzing facts and technical information, but also considering their feelings and the emotions of others when making decisions. Feelings and emotions play a key role in the decision-making process. A leader's ability to understand the questions, concerns, and their staff's commitment level before launching a new initiative will likely determine its success.

5. **Self-Management:** One of the seven principles of positive psychology identified by Shawn Achor in his book, *The Happiness Advantage*, is called the Zorro Circle. Research suggests leaders must be able to control everything within a small circle around themselves first before they can expect to have a positive impact on their organization or culture. Leaders who are skilled at self-management have a positive impact on culture.

6. **Positive Influence:** Successful leaders must be able to influence the moods and emotions of others in a positive way, and create a work environment where people can find productive ways of responding to challenges and obstacles. These leaders are empowering to work with and easily motivate those around them.

We have all heard that culture trumps strategy. To cultivate a thriving culture, we should focus on developing and honing our emotional intelligence skills, and reflecting on every time we have an opportunity to demonstrate our skills.

Summary

Let's not confuse science with "scientism." There are others that still may think emotional intelligence is a fad. However time and time again we learn that leaders who are attuned to others' emotions have high levels of self-awareness, demonstrate empathy, and control their own emotions are more successful in developing thriving school cultures. In the remaining chapters of this book we will examine the emotional intelligence behaviors and practices of highly skilled leaders.

Reflection

1. Describe a time when your emotions prevented you from having a successful interaction with a staff member or parent. What could you have done differently?

2. Describe a leader you worked with that had high levels of emotional intelligence. What characteristics and behaviors stood out?

3. Describe a leader you worked with who had low levels of emotional intelligence. What characteristics and behaviors stood out?

Steps to Improve your Emotional Intelligence

1. One of the first steps for improving emotional intelligence is becoming emotionally literate. In a journal, identify the different emotions you experience at work during the week. List the events that solicited the emotion. Did your emotions prevent you from being successful at work?

2. During the week, observe your staffs' emotions during interactions and in meetings. See if you are able to recognize when your staff experiences happiness, stress, or anger. Interact with a staff member who may not be having a good day. See if you are able to demonstrate empathy or help the person feel better.

CHAPTER 5
Emotional Self-Awareness

"If your emotional abilities aren't in hand, if you don't }have self-awareness, if you are not able to manage your distressing emotions, if you can't have empathy and have effective relationships, then no matter how smart you are, you are not going to get very far."

Daniel Goleman

In this chapter we will discuss the origins, range, and importance of emotions as well as how to identify them. Most important, we will begin our discussions on how you can gain control over your emotions and learn to use them for increasing your productivity, relationships, and satisfaction with life.

Origins of Emotions

Much more than just our feelings, emotions are sources of valuable information (Palmer, 2003.) Emotions may seem to suddenly "appear," but they are actually products of thoughts and experiences. Refusing to acknowledge emotions and lacking the ability to explore them present many problems for school leaders. Conversely, leaders who recognize emotions and can predict their sources will be prepared to deal with the challenges of leading a school.

One of the best explanations of how emotions work comes from a story first told by Dr. Joseph LeDoux, a New York University professor who was one of the pioneers in studying emotions. Most of us know how we would respond to seeing a rattlesnake as we were leisurely working in our garden. Startled and scared, we would feel our heart rate jump and our breathing increase rapidly. We would experience a "fight or flight" response or an "emotional hijacking." During an emotional hijacking we may not be at our best in communicating, thinking, or responding because the amygdala, the part of the brain that controls emotion, would have triggered the emotions of fight or flight. The fight or flight response is an evolutionary adaptation that helps species survive predation; as soon as an animal perceives danger, all its bodily systems are on high alert to battle the predator or escape it. Totally focused on survival, the amygdala sacrifices accuracy for speed. Thus, the amygdala has a tough time differentiating a real threat from a perceived threat. Both a rattlesnake and a stick that looks like a rattlesnake stimulate the amygdala and trigger the same fight or flight response. Our brains, as with other animals, are hardwired to produce all-out overreactions when we encounter a rattlesnake or a stick looking like a rattlesnake. Sometimes this works against us school leaders as we sort through the overabundance of messages on our computers and try to ascertain who has legitimate questions, who is making a sarcastic complaint about a decision we made, and who seems to be raising a serious problem but just needs us to listen.

The amygdala cannot distinguish rattlesnakes (real threats) from the hundreds of perceived threats a school leader faces regularly in the workplace. These perceived threats are often referred to as triggers. Triggers, and our emotional reactions to them, limit our success and cause most of the challenges we face in our administrative careers. Principals have identified such triggers as an upset parent on the phone, a staff member resisting change, and a call from the superintendent. When one of these triggers sets off the amygdala, our emotional reaction can resemble that of our picking up a rattlesnake.

Origins of Perceived Threats

Many of our perceived threats arise from childhood experiences, illogical thought patterns, or misperceptions that trigger our emotions. Can you recall an unpleasant childhood experience that still evokes a strong emotion today? Now, as an adult, when you are confronted with a similar event, do you experience a similar emotion? Thought patterns and misconceptions based on past experiences have shaped our present day mental models and paradigms and can be limiting factors to our success. The mental models themselves cannot limit success; it is our emotional reactions associated with them that determine our ability to lead. And whether a threat confronting us is real or perceived, our emotional reactions significantly impact our interactions with parents, students, and staff members. Have you ever reacted poorly to a staff member's question in a staff meeting? Was the staff member's question a real threat or a perceived threat? We need to understand that it is in our DNA to feel threatened. We are hardwired to perceive many threats and to react impulsively. This is what kept us alive in earlier times. However now, these perceived threats and impulsive reactions are what prevent us from having the relationships, success, and outcomes we desire.

During coaching sessions, many principals have shared that they have felt attacked and very uncomfortable in staff meetings. Old mental models of the need to defend themselves from attack set off their fight or flight responses, which then resulted in overreactions to the pressure. Even though these principals could cite numerous examples of legitimate questions and positive staff members, it is the negative experiences of the past that really control present day behavior of the principals. Again remember, we are hardwired to get defensive and react to perceived threats. To counter this, principals practiced challenging their mental models and reassured themselves that any teacher asking a question had a positive intention and was not mounting an attack. The few seconds it took to think this through delayed the amygdala from inappropriately providing the emergency response (the defensive overreaction), and the principals maintained composure. School leaders need to learn to "press pause", gather themselves, and be disciplined in their responses.

Understanding and perceiving your own emotions is perhaps the most important dimension of emotional intelligence. In addition to maintaining your composure and gaining respect in times of crisis, you model the importance of treating everyone with respect.

The Importance of Identifying Emotions

The following case studies and examples demonstrate the importance of leaders being able to identify their feelings. Not doing so prevents one from building bridges with teachers, parents, and community stakeholders and from having vital information needed to make good decisions; and it creates unhealthy, stressful situations. As you read the case studies that follow, see if there is any behavior to which you can relate.

E + R = O

For 10 years, John has been a principal of a high performing school in an influential suburban district. Parents call him weekly to ask about a detention, a grade on a test, playing time in a team sport, or some other event that is "a matter of life or death" to the parent but only trivial to John.

Although John understands the difficulty parents have in remaining objective when their child is involved, he usually becomes frustrated by the amount of time he needs to spend talking to parents about such issues. During his early years as principal, his frustration led to anger and at times caused him to react negatively to parents. Through coaching, John realized he was not happy with the outcomes of his conversations with parents and that he was responsible.

If we are not satisfied with the outcomes in our life we need to examine our own responses to the events. A great strategy for doing this is applying E + R = O. This success formula, inspired by the work of Jack Canfield and Brian and Tim Kight is one of the most important strategies to apply every day at work and in your personal life. The E stands for Event, the R for Response and the O equals Outcome. We often cannot control or change the events in our life. However, our outcomes will depend on our responses to these events. Some responses are disciplined, purposeful, and thoughtful and lead to great outcomes. Other reactions (not responses) are impulsive and irrational and lead to poor outcomes. What is even more alarming, as leaders, our responses or reactions become others' events! We need to be in more control and not let our emotions hijack us so we can get the outcomes that we desire.

But John now thinks of himself as an emotionally intelligent principal. When John notices his pulse or respiration increasing, his hands getting sweaty, or that knot in his stomach, he stops and separates his thoughts from his feelings. He presses pause and gathers himself. He realizes he is experiencing an event and wants to make an appropriate response. He knows to ask himself, "What am I thinking, and what am I feeling?" John also identifies what actions may have evoked his emotion and then reflects on whether, in the long run, sharing this emotion will help or hurt him in carrying out his responsibilities. John has learned how critical his awareness of his emotions is to his leadership success.

Managing one's emotions and controlling them are slightly different. Emotional self-control is related to how you control your emotions or reactions when you perceive a threat. Emotional self-management has to do with how effectively you manage your stress and moods. Emotional self-control can be one of the most challenging dimensions of the emotional intelligence construct.

As is well known, it is easier to keep the peace than to restore it; but this may not be true when dealing with emotions. Unless we work hard at using our skills and strategies to understand our emotions, they can get the best of us. There is little hope for the principal who is not able to maintain stability in times of conflict or crisis. There are times when school leaders are yelled at, distrusted, ignored, talked about, and made to feel insignificant—and this by their own staffs! While I always believed that the classroom teacher's job is the most demanding and exhausting job in education, my experiences as a teacher, administrator, and school leaders' coach showed me that there is no job in education filled with more stress, frustration, and challenges than that of the school principal or superintendent.

One of my professors used to say, "You have to have the skin of an armadillo and the heart of a marshmallow" to be an effective school leader. The armadillo skin symbolizes a level of protection to prevent your feelings from being hurt, which can cause you to overreact when emotional. A principal with the ability to maintain composure during emotional and intense situations will certainly gain the respect of a majority of staff members. Administrators regularly confirm the validity of the armadillo skin analogy and say that the thick skin develops as one serves as an administrator, and that without it, they would have lost confidence and self-esteem. I caution you to not protect or shield yourself from your own emotions but rather to become a successful administrator by controlling your emotions.

Nonproductive thought patterns

The following example shows how previously held thought patterns can prevent our brain cortex from using logic while allowing the aymgdala to trigger an emotion leading to a poor reaction.

I often ask educators at conferences, "What would be your first thoughts if the fire alarm went off? Fear? Stress?" Most educators respond by saying fear; however, fear (and stress) are not thoughts, but emotions. The amygdala first associates the fire alarm with danger and puts us in action mode to flee the danger. I then ask, "If during this presentation you saw behind me a firefighter working on the fire alarm and it goes off, what would your thoughts be?" Many respond "not to worry; it's not real." Once again, in just nanoseconds, a previously held thought pattern associating someone working on an alarm with the sounds of a fire alarm triggers our emotion (relief). We have many previously held thought patterns that make us successful and productive. However, we also have some that jeopardize our rational decision-making responses and emotional well-being.

Identifying possible triggers

One of the best strategies for controlling your emotions is to identify possible triggers that could cause you to become emotionally hijacked. Triggers may be behaviors, language, people, or events that evoke an emotion. Based on a past experience, a traumatic incident, or a bad relationship, triggers likely cause a fight or flight response. If you know ahead of time what your triggers are, you can be prepared to practice another emotionally intelligent strategy and control your emotions. Even though your amygdala may once again sacrifice accuracy for speed, you will have already recognized that the perceived threat is not a real threat. You may now pause, presume positive intentions, use Stop-Look-Listen or other strategies, and successfully control your emotions. When I do workshops for schools or leadership preparation programs, in one activity each participant is asked to identify three of his or her own triggers. Most frequently, group members' triggers are phone calls from parents, calls from the central office, a particular teacher openly questioning a decision, someone showing up late for a meeting, and attendees not paying attention in meetings.

Presume positive intentions.

During the last decade, no reform initiative tested school leaders' emotional intelligence more than implementing new teacher evaluation systems. Emotions from teachers were flying high across the country and principals were being asked to do something that some felt they had little time or adequate skill to do. Rick, a middle school principal, was one of those principals.

From coaching, Rick learned that before making decisions or reacting in times of uncertainty or conflict, it's best to search his feelings, analyze viable options that would produce his desired outcome, and then take action. Rick proved that as difficult as it is to change behaviors, with practice and committed effort, it can be done.

Rick had shared a story illustrating how his illogical thoughts or not presuming positive intentions tended to cause him to become angry. After he observed one of his new, aspiring teachers teach a great lesson, Rick completed a positive evaluation with a few suggestions for improvement. Although teachers have an opportunity to write comments on the evaluation, most teachers usually just thank him and sign the form. But in this particular situation, the teacher did not.

Rick said, "She asked if she could take the observation, keep it for a day or so, and re-read it, and I said, 'Sure.' I almost took it as, 'Does she not trust me?' This is something I really need to work on. I don't know how you get past assuming you know what teachers are thinking or what their motives are. I assumed the reason she wanted to read this further is because she really doesn't trust me and that I might have put something bad in there."

Although no teacher had ever disagreed with an evaluation he had given, when the teacher wanted to take the evaluation home, he jumped to the conclusion "Something must be wrong," which led to his anger. When we separate our thoughts from our feelings, we can usually identify the reason for our emotions, and we are primed to make better decisions. Rick later learned he could have separated his feelings and thoughts and asked himself for any positive reasons why the person might have wanted to read over the evaluation. The strategy of presuming positive intentions can often prevent an emotional hijacking.

How to Identify Your Emotions

Now that you know how important it is to identify your emotions, how do you go about it? The most important part of the process sounds simple, but it requires discipline. Take the time to explore why you are feeling what you are feeling—stop, look, and listen. Emotion is sometimes thought of as E(nergy in) MOTION. Self-reflection at that point may seem like the hardest thing in the world to do, but it becomes easier with practice. When you feel an emotion, identify why the feeling is there. Why do you feel sad, angry, or happy? If you decide the emotion is anger, then ask yourself, "Why anger? Did someone intentionally cause this, is there a real threat, or has the amygdala sacrificed accuracy for speed yet again?"

If the threat is real, you will need to manage your emotions and choose an effective strategy for de-escalating the situation. As the leader of an emotionally intelligent culture, you cannot afford to inappropriately react to people upset with you, and you can use the opportunity to model the behavior you want your school to exhibit.

Strategies for slowing down the urge to lash out and giving yourself time to choose wisely could include taking deep breaths, counting to ten, asking to continue the conversation later, or communicating that you have hurt feelings. And even if the other person has initiated the confrontation, you must take responsibility for renewing contact with the person and clearing the air.

More than once in my career, when I have explained in a calm, rational manner how a colleague has hurt my feelings by making some comment, the colleague has shared that he or she was feeling angry and upset about something else entirely and has apologized. Nearly every time this has happened, a productive, healing dialogue has followed. In contrast, early in my career as a principal, before studying emotional intelligence, I spent a vast amount of time repairing relationships I had broken with my sharp tongue.

Reflection

1. Think about a time during a school day when you overreacted to someone's comments. Might your overreaction have been caused by something that had happened earlier in the day and was totally unrelated to this particular conversation? What were you feeling at the time of the first incident? What were you thinking at the time of the second incident?

2. Record incidents from the last year to which you reacted negatively and ones to which you responded appropriately. Identify what triggered both the positive and negative behaviors. For the positive responses, what helped you respond appropriately? Were the triggers for negative reactions different from the triggers for positive responses?

3. Practice pausing and identifying your feelings during intense situations.

4. Record these practices in a journal. Notice your learning curve: is it a smooth straight upward curve, or are there dips in it as you learn more about the nuances of improving your self-control?

5. Identify your triggers that evoke negative emotions. Beside each trigger, identify a strategy that you would like to practice when the trigger happens.

6. Typically, when you get upset or angry about something, how long does it take you to calm yourself? Do you always realize you are angry or upset?

7. Do you recall ever making an important decision while you were emotionally hijacked? Did it turn out to be a good or bad decision?

8. Are there certain times of the day you experience more stress or frustrations than others? If so, what do you usually do when you become aware you are stressed and frustrated?

Steps to Improve Your Emotional Self-Awareness

1. Take time during the day or week to explore your feelings and thoughts. Try to differentiate between the two. Increase your vocabulary related to emotions by writing words that best describe your feelings (not thoughts).

2. When an event occurs that creates stress or conflict for you, explore the strength of your emotions during the event. Identify the fundamental emotion that was evoked in you. How strong was the emotion? What behavior resulted from the emotion? Was the behavior impulsive? Can you connect it to your past in any way? Were you able to stop, look, and listen? Did you use another strategy to buy yourself some time to avert the fight or flight response?

3. With a trusted colleague, share what your feelings were during the day of the event in question 2 above. Differentiate between feelings and thoughts during your discussion.

CHAPTER 6
Authenticity

"Authenticity is the alignment of head, mouth, heart, and feet—thinking, saying, feeling, and doing the same thing—consistently. This builds trust, and followers love leaders they can trust."

Lance Secretan

This chapter discusses the importance of principals learning to appropriately express their emotions, the spectrum of emotional behaviors, coaching strategies for helping you express your feelings, and suggestions for times when it is NOT appropriate to express your feelings.

Engaging Hearts and Minds

In Buckingham's (1999) groundbreaking work *First Break All the Rules: What Great Managers Do Differently*, the author identified 12 key questions to which an organization's staff must be able to answer "yes" to qualify as having a culture of excellence.

1. Do I know what is expected of me at work?

2. Do I have the materials I need to do my work?

3. Do I have the opportunity to do what I do best every day?

4. In the last seven days have I received praise?

5. Does my principal or someone at work care about me?

6. Does someone at work encourage my professional development?

7. Do my opinions matter?

8. Does my school's mission make my job feel important?

9. Are my coworkers committed?

10. Do I have a best friend at work?

11. In the last six months has someone talked to me about my progress or given me feedback?

12. Do I have opportunities to learn and grow or for advancement? (p. 28)

It is every leaders' goal to have staff members engaged. Keeping this list near your desk as a friendly reminder will remind you of the strategies for developing a thriving culture.

Accountable to Each Other

An emotionally intelligent principal recognizes and praises the work of students and staff members. The quick jump from good to great that our school made was well-documented. When I was a principal, despite having one of the lowest per pupil expenditures in the state, we ranked among the best in student achievement and value-added qualities. Trying to find our "magic formula" for success, schools from all over the state visited our campus. Although many best practices and a relentless focus on student learning were apparent, many school personnel saw something else. Visitors would comment, "We knew your school was high on collaboration and in using data, but we were surprised by the evident real caring about one another that is present." Cultivating such a culture starts with the principal, but it doesn't stop there. A principal's sharing love for the school and the happiness and pride the students bring him or her is a great model for the rest of the community. However, it was the fact that we all held each other accountable for the way we talked to and treated each other. We were also good at praising each other and recognizing effort and outcomes. The missing piece in many schools is being authentic with each other, yet holding each other to the collective commitments made to one another.

Positive Outcomes of Sharing Emotions

Sharing emotions helps a principal be a leader and builds trust and respect in the school community. At your school, once you have shared your emotions of excitement about achieving goals or disappointment over not having achieved them, the achievement or lack thereof is then "official." One of the most significant findings of behavioral change research to surface recently is the importance of establishing and recognizing emotions. Years of hospital-related research reveals that regardless of the disease diagnosed and behavior modification necessary to add longevity, many patients return to old habits, even if it means a shorter life. But when doctors talk to patients about changing behaviors to allow for being there when their child gets married, experiencing the birth of their first grandchild, and playing with their grandchildren, the positive emotions associated with the change are more successful. Nutritionists and dietitians have learned most people's success with diet plans is not based on the logic of maintaining a balance between calories consumed and burned, but the emotions based on looking and feeling thinner and on surviving to experience more of life. Rather than using logic to drive and lead change, some schools are tapping into the emotions and hopes of a school community in which all teachers can collaborate and feel safe. Identifying, communicating, and using emotions are necessary tools to cultivate the culture you want.

When I speak to school leaders, I often show a clip of the 1961 movie *Spartacus* starring Kirk Douglas and Tony Curtis after this brief introduction:

Born into slavery during the Roman Empire and gladiator era, Spartacus learned to fight and was given food, clothing, and a good life (for a slave) at a gladiator camp. In the movie, the gladiator, Spartacus (Kirk Douglas) leads a revolution in which gladiators escape their camp and go village to village releasing more slaves. Their goal is to reach the coast, gain the help of pirates, and sail to freedom in a new land. As they journey on, Spartacus and his troops continue to triumph in battles with trained Roman armies. At the movie's end, after pirates betray Spartacus and his troops, several Roman troops surround Spartacus and the few surviving gladiators. The Roman commander, in an effort to identify Spartacus from the remaining slaves or slain bodies, offers the slaves a chance to escape death and return to the life of slavery by identifying Spartacus. Otherwise, all the slaves would be crucified along the road back to Rome. As Spartacus begins to stand to identify himself, every slave, one by one, stands and says, "I am Spartacus."

The movie clip is inspirational and models an emotionally intelligent workplace. At first, caught up in the bravery and loyalty displayed to Spartacus, many people think the clip is modeling a high level of commitment to a leader. But the clip is about something much more complex than commitment to a leader. It was not the fear of starvation, crucifixion, slavery, or death that enabled Spartacus and his troops to win so many battles against the Roman Empire or make their last stand on the hillside, it was the hope of freedom and a better life. We have known for years that fear is not a productive motivator over time. However, fear is the emotion that most leaders tap into when leading reform or change, intentional or not. Leaders, however, could tap into emotions associated with hope and what our school could be. Capturing the hearts and minds of others is key to leading transformation and change.

If it's a workshop, following the film clip, I like to do a Hopes and Fears activity. On large poster board, participants write one to three fears, ones that will be barriers to the changes they want to take place or ones that prevent them from making necessary changes. Then, reading aloud many of the fears, I acknowledge that they are real. I also remind them that courage is not the absence of fear, but the ability to overcome their fears. I encourage the principals to use a whole professional development session to explore each fear and not to dismiss or play down any fear. Next, I ask the participants to write the hopes for their school if everyone involved could make the necessary changes to fulfill the hope. Just like in the Spartacus clip, it will be the hopes for a better place that will be the intrinsic motivator for change. By posting the hopes and referring to them often, you will reinforce the vision with staff members.

Empathy, The Most Important Skill.

Mike, a school principal, was not chosen as principal of a new building, much to his surprise and dismay. On the "fast track" to becoming a principal at the age of 29, Mike had always been recognized as an outstanding teacher and leader. When the superintendent told him he needed to improve his leadership skills to become a strong candidate for future promotions, he felt overlooked and undervalued. A few weeks later, Mike decided to take an emotional intelligence assessment and participate in emotional intelligence coaching. He shared that he usually tried to hide his youth and lack of worldly experience by personifying an image of toughness and strength rather than empathy or caring. During his professional training as a young principal, he had learned principals were more effective if they had a backbone and did not display emotions. "And empathy was the worst of all emotions." Mike's lack of empathy prevented him from connecting with his staff and parents in the community.

Another video clip that I like to use during presentations features Ronald Reagan addressing the nation following the space shuttle Challenger disaster. This clip mesmerizes the audience, and many people remember exactly what they were doing when Challenger exploded. The first purpose of this clip is to show an example of Reagan, "The Great Communicator," connecting and displaying empathy to the nation, and the second is to show how powerful emotions are. The reason people can usually remember what they were doing and where they were is that the accident evoked very strong emotions. I discuss with teachers that although many of the changes they experienced during their career were not as devastating as the Challenger tragedy, every change or reform initiative in their career probably evoked strong emotions that even now cause them to recall the time of change. Once you understand the depth and power of emotions, you can empathize with what your staff must go through to adopt new practices. When principals initiate reforms, teachers usually have to abandon some habit, practice, or belief to which they have been deeply attached. The change is loss, and this moves people very quickly out of their comfort zones. Expressing empathy during this time and reminding people of the support you plan to provide is critical for success.

Expressing Emotions

One of the biggest barriers to expressing emotions is understanding that it is okay to emote. People will recognize and appreciate the strengths of a leader who has the ability to express his or her emotions in a productive manner and does not overreact, causing rifts in relationships that later take time and energy to rebuild.

A barrier to expressing emotions is the myth that showing emotions equates to softness. One common mistake is confusing soft skills with a soft person or an emotionally intelligent leader as a soft person. Having good listening skills, being attentive to people's emotions, and effectively expressing your own emotions do not make people soft. You can be emotionally intelligent and have a backbone.

Coaching Tips for Expressing Emotions

As you practice expressing your emotions, it is important to be sincere and not manipulative. I once worked for a leader who sent a letter to his staff only when he needed something in return. Although I believed his letter was sincere, because this was the only time he ever took the time to share his emotions, the staff viewed the letter as a form of manipulation, rather than a sincere reaching out to them. Be careful not to use emotions to control, manipulate, or gain an advantage over people but rather to connect with them for mutual benefit.

Separate thoughts and feelings. One principal showed very high emotional intelligence in recognizing that sharing disappointment instead of anger would nurture his school community and position members for future improvement. Sharing anger can give you a quick release of frustration; but in the long run, it makes others quick to blame each other so someone else can be in the path of the consequences of your anger. Strong leaders do not shame, name, or blame others.

Jim, a middle school principal, is driven and has high expectations for his staff and students. For three years in a row, his building has received an excellent rating by the state department of education. Jim eagerly anticipated seeing student achievement scores and could hardly wait the three months for the release of the results. When the test results finally came to the school, Jim was disappointed. Because the scores were lower than in the past, the school would lose its excellent rating. Disappointed and angry, Jim's first thoughts were, "Why did the staff let me down?" But quickly separating his thoughts from his feelings, Jim realized that the students and staff would be just as disappointed as he.

In this case study, Jim's thoughts that the staff had let him down led to his feelings of sadness and anger. Recognizing that his thoughts were driving his emotions, he paused. He then replaced his first thought with the thought that his students and staff would be greatly disappointed; he let this second thought drive his behavior of displaying empathy and concern. Jim addressed the staff and told them that he recognized how hard everyone had worked to continue the outstanding history of success they had achieved over the last few years. He then informed the staff that this year's results were not as good and that the school would lose its excellent rating. The staff could easily see that Jim was not angry, but truly disappointed for the staff and teachers, as well as for himself. Jim expressed his feelings of sadness and disappointment at seeing the test results. He expressed his concern for how the public might respond, but more specifically his concern about informing the student body that the test goals had not been met. By openly sharing his emotions in an appropriate manner, Jim connected with his staff more on this day than he had the three years prior when the school had met their state test goals. Jim had learned how to effectively express his emotions.

Write notes of appreciation. Writing notes to staff, students, and parents thanking them for their efforts when something goes well is a good practice; don't ever take for granted that they automatically know you appreciate them. In addition to writing notes, principals must also encourage and provide resources for teachers to write notes to one another.

One year we gave all of our teachers dippers, buckets, and note cards shaped as water drops. It was our goal to frequently fill each others' buckets with positive notes, praise, or feedback. If someone witnessed someone sharing negative comments, we would politely ask him or her not to dip water out of our buckets. We also had custom-printed praise cards that made it simple for staff members to write notes to one another. When a staff member received letters from the principal and peers frequently during the year, there was a culture of caring, support, and encouragement.

For more than a decade, I had been fortunate to work for a superintendent who cultivated a family atmosphere in our district by making time for teachers, visiting school buildings, and frequently writing letters and e-mails of sincere appreciation. Most recently I worked for an executive director who prioritized time each week to write positive, warm handwritten notes to staff and others. His handwritten notes (sometimes very hard to read) were one of the most appreciative gifts and recognition I received, even more valuable than end of year bonuses. Frequently writing notes, especially handwritten notes, is a powerful strategy for connecting with others.

Watch body language. Research of common experience makes it clear that facial expressions and body language communicate emotions. One of the most impressive presentations I have ever seen was in Malaga, Spain, by Dr. Harold True, who made hundreds of films of facial expressions, each lasting nanoseconds. During his presentation, he showed video in which he morphed different expressions of the eyes, mouth, and different parts of the face. I realized how powerful our body language and facial expressions are in communicating accurately or sending mixed messages about our emotions. Although they could see only parts of a face, people were amazingly accurate in reading emotions.

We have all heard that crossing your arms when someone is talking can send the message that you are not open to what the other person is suggesting. It is important to be aware that your countenance, body position, and physical habits are sending messages about what you are feeling, regardless of your words.

Conflict resolution through e-mail. Another coaching tip for emotional expression is to avoid expressing negative emotions through e-mail. Although a necessary tool, e-mail can create substantial problems if overused, especially for resolving conflicts. We all have sent or misread an e-mail that led to more problems. Try picking up the phone, or better yet, schedule a face-to-face meeting.

Sharing emotions. Tom was a new principal who rarely expressed his emotions. In spite of his organizational skills, instructional leadership skills, and management skills, he struggled to communicate with his staff. As part of his emotional intelligence development, he made a point of expressing in his opening day presentation that he understood and shared in his staff's excitement about and pride in achieving an "Excellent" rating. As he spoke, he smiled, stood tall, and clapped during the conversation about the rating. He went on to express his disappointment about the failure of the operating levy at the polls. At a coaching session, he shared the noticeable improvement in connection he felt with the staff; he told of several staff members noting a difference in him that day. As leaders, we often confuse strong and stable with not showing or expressing emotions. A principal's strength and stability is not threatened by the expression of his or her emotions. In fact, people regard leadership skills as more impressive if they include the ability to express feelings appropriately.

Being fair. Nothing can jeopardize a leader's influence more than perceptions of having favorites or not being impartial. But the truth is every leader will have staff with whom they are closest. Rather than ignoring it, acknowledge these people as your support system and communicate to your staff that these relationships will not impact the fairness and equity of treatment of staff. One of my favorite video clips on this topic is from Daniel Pink. It was a clip sharing how monkeys would get either cucumbers or grapes for doing a task correctly. Monkeys do like cucumbers, but they love grapes. When the monkey would see another monkey get a grape after it had received a cucumber for doing the same task, it would become frustrated and angry. There are times in our own workplace where we have felt that others received grapes while we received cucumbers. The same goes for your staff, too. Some of them think you are giving grapes to others, while they are stuck with cucumbers.

Following my first year as principal, my teachers completed a survey to provide feedback on my first year. I have always perceived feedback of any kind as a gift. The instrument provided feedback to me about how I was perceived as an instructional leader, manager, supporter, and coach; it rated my organizational skills and visibility, and my ability to maintain direction and set a vision. One of my lowest ratings was on favoritism. When I reviewed the results of the assessment with the staff, rather than becoming angry or defensive about the staff's perception that I had favorites, I acknowledged that I do have favorites. However, I pointed out that I did allow every staff member who needed to leave early or come in late to do so, that I had covered classes for almost every teacher, and that all their budgets were the same. I explained my belief that there is a difference between equity and fairness and levels of relationships. I explained my tendency to talk and spend more time with teachers who, like me, were willing to openly share emotions as we talked. I pointed out that I seemed to converse with people who did not always agree with me, but who liked to debate, dialogue, and examine educational issues. I shared my goal of addressing this perception and building high quality relationships with all my staff members. Amazingly enough, addressing this concern and openly inviting deeper levels of conversation, including the sharing of emotions, improved all our staff relationships.

Remember, courage is not the absence of fear, but triumph over fear. I was not afraid to address a concern or a negative perception. And during the conversation, staff members came to view me as not just their principal, but as a fellow human being, who, like them, is capable of having different levels of relationships with different people without jeopardizing equity and fairness.

When Not to Share Emotions

Although people want to be led by leaders who have feelings, principals should explore their emotions and decide what impact sharing their emotions will have on the school culture during an event or situation. There certainly will be times when it is not appropriate to share your emotions. A principal can make this determination by reflecting on the outcome sharing an emotion will have on their staff, students, or parents. The issue is not that expressing too many emotions can have a detrimental effect on your leadership as much as the importance of demonstrating stability.

Once I worked with an administrator who often used his emotions to manipulate the staff. Whenever there was a situation in which he felt the staff perceived him as ineffective, he would play the emotion card. Sharing family issues or challenges, he sought empathy from the staff. Although the strategy worked for a year or two, the staff eventually began to feel manipulated and trust issues arose.

As mentioned earlier, you can express your emotions without being overly emotional. I recall watching a principal address his staff about a situation in which he felt a lack of support. He reminded his staff that during his 20-year tenure, he had supported and encouraged them to take risks outside their comfort zones. Although the principal was angry and disappointed about the events that had occurred, he never let his emotions get the best of him. He communicated his disappointment and his previous anger; he did not display it. Mirroring the principal's stability and calmness and listening attentively, the staff appreciated the principal sharing his feelings and committed to doing a better job of supporting him in the future.

Reflection

1. Would your staff describe you as a person who effectively and appropriately expresses your emotions? Why or why not?

2. Think about a time recently that you have expressed your emotions to a staff member. Were the emotions positive or negative? Are you better at expressing positive or negative emotions? Are you better at expressing your emotions to certain staff members, or are you able to express your emotions in front of the entire staff?

3. Have you ever considered a school leader weak for expressing emotions? Why or why not?

Steps to Improve Your Authenticity

1. Take time each day to express an emotion to a trusted colleague.

2. Write a sincere thank you note in which you communicate a feeling.

3. Ask a colleague after a meeting or event in which you spoke or made a presentation whether you effectively expressed any emotions.

4. Reflect on how you may have used your tone of voice, facial expression, or body language during a meeting or event. Get feedback from a trusted colleague.

CHAPTER 7
Awareness of Others

"Awareness of others is a beautiful thing. Learning how to support and encourage, and stopping long enough to pay attention to someone other than yourself is a truly beautiful quality."

India de Beaufort

People do not quit their jobs; they quit their bosses, according to an old maxim. It follows then, that in education the 50 percent of teachers who leave the field within their first five years are leaving their principals, not education. While I am not ready to accept this assumption, I do believe that a principal's level of support, encouragement, and mentoring during a teacher's initial experiences is critical.

If principals were more aware of and sensitive to teachers' emotions, they would offer more encouragement and support. And for the many principals leading their schools through change, the ability to perceive and understand the emotions of others may be the most valuable skill of all.

Emotional Intelligence Empowers School Leaders

Understanding others' emotions provides you with valuable leadership information. When you understand the emotions people are experiencing, and when you don't understand them, if you take the time to explore the thoughts and reasons behind the emotions, your awareness of the realities of your school community will increase. With this information you will have your hand on the pulse and know when it is time to be persistent and when it is time to be patient.

Cultivating a Culture of Commitment

If you accept the challenge of understanding what your staff is feeling, then you can cultivate what I call a "culture of commitment." This culture will enable you to successfully manage resistance and directly deal with noncompliance, which is essential if you, your staff, and your students are to achieve the school's mission. Just as important, when you display an understanding of your staff's emotions, your staff will reciprocate and work hard at understanding your emotions as well. Not only does it strengthen everyone's feeling of community, the quality of work that takes place in such a school is amazing.

After reading much of Richard DuFour's work, I have avoided using the word *build* or *develop* when discussing or coaching about culture. Cultures are like gardens and not like buildings (DuFour & Burnette, 2002). Gardens need watering, weeding, fertilizing, and constant care as compared to buildings that may need periodic maintenance. In fact, most homeowners and architects would be annoyed or frustrated to build a structure that needed the same attention as a garden. But cultures built on trust, respect, and high commitment to excellence are more like gardens than anything else. The failure to accurately portray the necessary work to "maintain the garden" in preparing leaders has led to much of the frustration they face when trying to build rather than cultivate their school cultures.

Addressing Noncompliance

Failing to address staff members not in compliance with the school mission or school processes is a huge mistake for school leaders. Although school leaders may rationalize that their inactions on this problem are "keeping the peace" or not "rocking the boat," they are doing just the opposite. By failing to acknowledge staff members' not honoring commitments and not following through on tasks important to student and school success, the principal is sowing toxic weeds instead of removing them from the garden. Do not confuse patience with procrastinating or refusing to deal with noncompliance. This is detrimental to the overall success of the school and displays fear rather than courage.

Confusing Noncompliance with Resistance

Another mistake that principals low in emotional intelligence make is confusing noncompliance with resistance. Resistance is more closely related to the ultimate goal of commitment than people realize and is not noncompliance, which is actual nonconformance to requirements. I try to learn from the questions that resisters ask; their questions help me know how to refine my communication of the goal as well as force me to think about every aspect and impact of a decision. Leaders should embrace resistance. To revisit our gardening analogy, when staff members ask questions about the fertilizer, the need for watering, why they are growing certain plants, or even imply they are not excited about horticulture, the principal cannot confuse this with noncompliance. Even in the face of resistance, you have to believe in your teachers' professionalism, and that each staff member will till and nurture the garden. When principals confuse resistance with noncompliance, they create barriers to performance and drain staff members' motivation.

I often share this same mistake I made in my first year as principal in a newly configured middle school with new teachers from three different buildings. From day one, our school attempted to be cutting edge. Voting not to follow the teacher association's contract, our school created larger classes for advanced students and smaller classes for struggling students. During the first year the teachers also gave up their 30 minutes of uninterrupted lunch so I could trade a few aide positions for an additional teacher. Not all teachers agreed with this, nor did they all have a positive attitude about it, but everyone was compliant and fulfilled their jobs as professionals. I remember we were exploring new territory our first year and challenging nearly every paradigm of how schools are traditionally organized to create a new and successful school. Many times the teachers asked legitimate questions or expressed fears about our journey. Unfortunately for them, I was just starting my emotional intelligence development, and I was not as skilled as I am today in understanding others' emotions. Sometimes thinking of their very important questions and fears as just poor attitude, I failed to acknowledge and value their behavior of fulfilling everything we did to the best of their ability. That first year was much more difficult than it needed to be for the adults in the building, but our newly designed school created instant and never-before-achieved success for our students. I apologized to my staff for my lack of understanding of their emotions during their first year of reform. On the positive side, we all discussed how much we had grown professionally and personally after our first year.

Focus on Behaviors Rather than Attitudes

An example of focusing on attitudes rather than behaviors is provided by some of my interactions with Mrs. Williams. Mrs. Williams was one of the most outstanding, patient, caring, and veteran teachers in our building, however, she and I had a few strong philosophical differences. Because I am a strong proponent of frequent assessments of learning, we had common assessments and short cycle assessments in every subject area. Not to be used for students' grades, these assessments provided information about what our students had not yet mastered or learned so our teachers could reteach, intervene, or provide other high quality, corrective instruction.

Before I completed my emotional intelligence training, I was often frustrated that Mrs. Williams' attitudes towards these assessments were different from my views. I was afraid she would influence the staff to view these assessments as unnecessary. Although she did an outstanding job of assessing for learning and designing intervention lessons and high-quality corrective instruction, she did not believe in the new assessment processes I had initiated and thought they were just a trend in an era of student accountability. As an ultimate professional and one of the district's best teachers, Mrs. Williams was 100 percent compliant with our school's process.

But, my focus on attitudes rather than behaviors caused problems in our relationship, and others took notice. Instead of using her as an outstanding role model (compliant to the school's mission and vision, even though she was not in total agreement), I created a situation where people walked on eggshells around us, and some of the younger teachers may have been thinking, "If I do not agree 100 percent with Dr. Moore, regardless of how much I follow through, our relationship may not be as strong as others." What a mistake I was making! And thank goodness for my emotional intelligence training. The truth is I have never agreed with 100 percent of any of the requests my bosses have made, but I have been compliant (most of the time). You see, a culture of commitment is not just about being committed to duties, it is more than that. It is being committed to one another. It is naïve to think we can create a culture in which everyone is 100 percent committed to everything we do. However, we can create a culture in which 100 percent of the people are committed to each other. Once people are committed to each other, some are compliant to initiatives or tasks out of respect to their peers; some, because they agree it is the right thing to do; some, because it fits a vision of professional behavior; and some are compliant because they feel they have to be. The more you focus and acknowledge the positive behaviors in your school, the more you will increase the positive attitudes and the higher level of commitment you will have. I have seen this transformation occur in several buildings.

Years later, Mrs. Williams and I have one of the best relationships, and I often bump into her in the community. My personal development has enabled me to appreciate all the gifts that she brought to our school. To this day we may still disagree on assessments and the era of accountability but are committed to each other.

Effectively Lead School Reform

Teachers inevitably will experience stress, anxiety, doubt, confusion, anger, and even resentment during the implementation stage of any new idea or strategy that inherently implies that what they are currently doing is not good enough or that they can do better. While school leaders can choose their words carefully as they explain the reasons behind new initiatives or school reforms, leaders need to be sensitive to and aware of their staffs' emotions, which are real and justified. As hard as it is to change behaviors and actions on one's own, it is even more challenging when someone imposes those changes.

As mentioned earlier, people actually go through a grieving process when asked to change or stop doing something to which they are accustomed. Someone once said that all human beings have two basic fears; (1) the fear that they will not be loved, and (2) the fear that they may not be good enough. This makes sense and can be applied to the challenges of school reform. Whenever you ask teachers to change behaviors or teaching strategies, recognize that a reaction some faculty will have is that of inadequacy—whatever their current approach, it isn't good enough.

If this is combined with a lack of trust or respect—perhaps when principals are new to the position—then the fear of not being loved surfaces. When principals recognize these two most common fears and show empathy, patience, care, and respect during any reform initiative, their schools will more successfully weather the change process.

Strategies for Understanding Others' Emotions

Collaborating on norms, exercising patience, developing timelines, controlling the emotional temperature, setting realistic expectations, and allowing your staff to experience their emotions are powerful strategies that emotionally intelligent leaders use.

Establish collaborative norms. Collaborative norms are rules or commitments people make to each other about how they will communicate, respond to conflict, and treat each other. Developing these norms is an important step in creating an emotionally intelligent school. After developing these norms, post them in the teachers' meeting area (or lounge) and identify one or two norms to practice in each staff meeting. In our school we selected these seven norms:

1. Pausing

2. Paraphrasing

3. Probing

4. Putting ideas on the table

5. Paying attention to self and others

6. Presuming positive intentions

7. Pursuing a balance between advocacy and inquiry

(adapted from the original work of Garmston & Wellman, (2009), *The Adaptive School: A Sourcebook for Developing Collaborative Groups* and Senge (1990), *The Fifth Discipline: The Art and Practice of the Learning Organization*).

Pausing, a powerful tool for improving emotional intelligence, is especially useful in meetings. Because teachers are always short on time, discussions at meetings can seem more like an Olympic ping-pong game than an opportunity to discuss and solve problems. We try to wait 3–5 seconds after a colleague speaks, so we can process and understand what he or she has said. Associated with the research on "wait time" exhibited by master teachers in the classroom, pausing relates to higher level thinking skills. At your next staff meeting, practice just this one norm. Although it is challenging, it improves the level of discussion.

Paraphrasing is the most powerful tool for reaching understanding and de-escalating conflict. Thinking Collaborative, an organization that focuses on maximizing professional collaboration, stresses not using the word "I" when paraphrasing another person. "What I hear you are saying is… ," is more about you and not the person speaking. Alternatives that move the focus to the speaker include, "So what you are saying is… ," or "So, the emotions you are feeling are…" I have used this skill numerous times when calming frustrated parents or coaching staff members.

Probing for specificity is digging deeper to really understand what a person is saying, thinking, or feeling. I usually use a "softener" and ask permission before probing for specificity. For example, "May I explore this a little further with you?" or "I sense your frustration here, but can you please share with me why you are so frustrated?"

Putting ideas on the table requires courage on the part of the speaker as well as acceptance, trust, and openness on the part of the group; if a culture encourages such behaviors, the power of synergy can create change. A strategy for this is "first turn-last turn." As we go around the table, everyone in turn adds a comment, thought, or idea. Use this power tool when you have one or two people dominating a conversation or meeting.

Paying attention to self and others is the essence of emotional intelligence. We need to be aware of and sensitive to everyone around the table. Although we may not agree with each other, we are committed to one another.

Presuming positive intentions is perhaps the most important and valuable norm in creating a high-functioning team and developing emotional intelligence. When we assure ourselves that no one will do anything to intentionally hurt us, we view things much differently without fear.

Balancing advocacy and inquiry is the last norm. Emotionally intelligent people care as much about what others are thinking and feeling as they do about advocating for their own thoughts and feelings. When a leader really starts to inquire into the thoughts, ideas, and feelings of others, a powerful culture emerges.

Many schools will thrive to cooperate rather than collaborate. This leads to "artificial harmony" of getting along with each other because they never openly engage in discussing controversies or disagreements. Highly functioning teams can debate and disagree respectfully.

Be patient and give a timeline. During a faculty meeting before the start of a school year, John, a new principal, introduced a schedule increasing students' academic time. In past years, teachers had built the schedule and forwarded it to the principal. The former schedule allotted teachers 45-minute lunches (the teacher contract stipulated a minimum 30 minutes for lunch) and assigned no duties during their planning periods, which allowed most teachers to grade papers or check e-mail. A major paradigm shift for the faculty was that planning time would now involve collaborating with peers in teams to share successful teaching strategies and analyze student work as they built a professional learning community, an important initiative of the new principal.

As soon as John communicated the plans, strategies, and vision of a new professional learning community, several teachers appeared to become frustrated and agitated. But John recognized their fear and communicated to the staff that fear is normal during the change process. John quickly shared how it took his previous building three years to become a professional learning community. Because he shared his perspective on the timeline, teachers could realize that they would have time to get used to the changes and grow into them, and that it was normal not being comfortable with the idea yet.

When principals initiate professional learning communities, they usually find that some teachers prefer working by themselves rather than as a member of a team, and some prefer working only with children. Others have no urge for further refinement or developing new skills. With such variables along with normal resistance, anger, fear, and sometimes even disrespect, the task of reform is challenging indeed.

Principals need to remember, as John did, that nearly every teacher is a dedicated, compassionate, professional educator. Never losing sight of this, John strived for a balance of persistence and patience during the implementation stages. He was patient because he understood the fear associated with change. He knew that for many people change is loss, and people actually have to go through a grieving process. So John displayed empathy and was sympathetic when he listened to concerns. However, persistently sharing research and data that supported the initiative, he is converting more and more faculty to his vision along the way. Now, several years later, teachers at John's high performing school embrace the concept of professional learning communities. In fact, the teachers build time for collaboration into the schedule. The strategies of being patient, sharing a timeline, being empathic about fear of change, but insistent on following the research-backed initiative are keys to success.

Control the temperature. Any school leader who overlooks the emotions of his or her staff and pushes on with a reform plan of the principal's own choosing, will indeed face failure. Heifetz and Linsky (2002) referred to the important skill of "controlling the temperature," or "monitoring the thermostat." When the school leader senses that emotions are rising, he or she needs to reclaim responsibility for tough issues by taking some responsibility away from the staff, establishing structure and roles, and addressing technical issues causing problems. During this time the school leader displays empathy and balances persistence with patience. When the temperature begins to lower, the school leader can once again give people responsibility in their comfort range, draw attention to tough issues, and bring conflicts to the surface.

Michele, the principal of a progressive middle school, demonstrated such leadership. For two years, during professional development time, Michele trained her teachers to use a new data management system to load assessments and use the system to grade, store, and sort data that would help identify students needing intervention. It was a great tool that contributed to the school's success. Unbeknownst to Michele, the district, excited about her building results, decided to integrate a district-wide data management system—a different system! So when teachers returned to school and learned that they were no longer able to use the system on which they had trained, frustration was rampant.

Teachers' stress level quickly rose with beginning-of-the-year activities, the reloading of their assessments onto a new system, and responsibility for new intervention planning. But Michele was reading the temperature. She quickly assumed responsibility for getting district personnel to reload all the assessments, and Michele scanned and ran all of the teachers' reports for the entire year. After the first half of the year, when the teachers felt comfortable with the new intervention program, Michele organized training sessions for teachers to learn the new data system. By the end of the year more than half of the staff had trained on the new system, and the rest trained during the summer. Michele had her hand on the thermostat, and when she sensed the temperature was getting hot, she turned it down until things stabilized. Not only is temperature control an important concept for administrators to learn, but once teachers understand the concept, they can communicate when they are feeling stressed.

Have realistic expectations. The school leader who thinks leading school reform will be easy and without emotions is over-romanticizing the world. If this book even suggests you can lead change without getting a bloody nose, then it has been misleading. Change is tough!

Allow staff to have their emotions. Many principals do not display negative emotions when asked to do a job—and they expect their staffs to act accordingly. Such leaders can be blindsided when staff show fear or discontent or become upset with decisions. My experience shows that many times when school leaders pick up on fear, anger, or sadness from teachers, they associate this with a lack of commitment from the staff causing the leaders to react negatively. They then spend more time sorting out the fact that the teachers' emotions were not equal to their commitment and then making up with the staff than they would have by just acknowledging emotions and moving forward. After reflection and concentrated effort on improving their emotional intelligence, school leaders can understand this chain of reactions and change their behaviors to reflect this new understanding. Fear, anger, and sadness are feelings that all people have, and expressing them is a right of staff as long as they are expressed appropriately. Any discomfort with those feelings that leaders have is their own problem. Never underestimate the value and importance of understanding the emotions of others.

Reflection

1. Think about a time when staff members may have thought you did not understand their emotions. Was this true? What could you have done to change those perceptions?

2. Have you ever been in a situation when someone did not understand how you were feeling? What were your thoughts at the time about this person? Is this how you want people to perceive you? What can you do to ensure that people know you are trying to understand their emotions?

3. Can you identify staff members in your building who are compliant rather than committed? Do you treat those people differently? When was the last time you addressed noncompliance in your building? How did you address the noncompliance?

Steps to Improve your Emotional Awareness of Others

1. Observe others in the workplace. Study their facial expressions, body language, and voices.

2. During an event at work try to be aware of what others are feeling. Do not be afraid to ask questions to confirm your perceptions.

3. After an event, compare observations with a colleague about others' emotions.

4. Try to walk in another person's shoes. Try to experience how that person feels.

CHAPTER 8
Emotional Reasoning

"Where we have strong emotions, we're liable to fool ourselves."

Carl Sagan

Every day principals make decisions, hundreds per day, five days a week. To make many of those decisions, information must be gathered quickly from a variety of sources. Today's schools are more data-driven than ever. When examining data, what information do principals gather about emotions? As mentioned earlier, refusing to acknowledge the emotions of those around you, including parents, teachers, and students, sets you up for a nonproductive tenure as a school leader.

Balancing Technical and Emotional Information

The development of national and state standards for school principals has narrowed the focus of the skills and abilities required for successful and effective school leaders. Principals must collect, sort, and analyze data from assessments, feedback, processes, piloted programs, and implementation of new strategies. There is tremendous pressure on principals to focus on state data, surveys, and achievement scores. While using hard data from these sources is paramount in creating successful schools, principals who ignore emotional information and fail to acknowledge the stress, fear, and anxiety associated with reform, new initiatives, and mandates will have little success in cultivating a culture of trust and commitment.

The principal in the following scenario piloted full inclusion in social studies and science classes, collecting data to support her position of using a full inclusion model throughout the school. Dana, the principal, has always been an advocate of full inclusion—placing students, regardless of their needs or disabilities, in regular classrooms with their peers. Although the social studies and science teachers had a more challenging year than usual, the student value-added and student achievement data showed the special education students were learning more in full inclusion social studies and science classrooms than in math and reading special education classes. The data were strong enough to support Dana's advocacy for inclusion, and she met with teachers at the year's end to plan implementing inclusion schoolwide the following year.

At the meeting, Dana listened as teachers expressed their concerns and their fears of moving from their traditional process of separating students with physical, mental, or behavioral challenges from regular classrooms. Although their students on IEPs in the pilot inclusion classes learned more than they had in years past, it was obvious that all of the teachers were scared, nervous, and even angry. The more teachers shared their frustrations and concerns, the more Dana listened. Many teachers lacked confidence in teaching students with special needs; all of them agreed it would be much more difficult to teach a variety of ability levels in their classrooms. Dana presumed positive intentions and knew deep down she did not have to convince teachers of the ethics of inclusion. She knew her priority at the time was not to influence, advocate, or debate, but rather to listen. When the meeting's designated ending time arrived, Dana thanked the teachers for sharing their concerns and expressing their feelings. But Dana said it was her responsibility to ensure high levels of learning for all students, and given the success of the pilot, the school would implement full inclusion the following year.

Next Dana asked the teachers to write their hopes and goals for all of the special education students in the building and what their vision was for full inclusion in their school. By focusing on the staff's hopes and vision, by introducing data that showed the special education students did learn more in a full inclusion environment, and by acknowledging the emotional information associated with the challenge of changing, Dana led the teachers in planning the successful implementation of a full inclusion model. As she collected the emotional data by listening carefully to her teachers, Dana realized how much she would need to support, encourage, and coach them through this process. Had Dana ignored the emotional data and underestimated the fear and resistance to the change, implementation of the model may have failed due to lack of buy-in from the teachers.

A balance between technical and emotional data collection and analyses may be the key to successfully implementing school reform initiatives. In the previous story, Dana knew what the right decision was. She also knew it was important to take in as much emotional information as she could to successfully plan for the implementation of full inclusion. By hearing and understanding the staff's level of fear associated with full inclusion, she could organize professional development and support around this new initiative. During the year, the teachers did struggle, and it was challenging. But at the end of the school year when the student data came back with higher-than-ever scores for students with disabilities and special needs, the school celebrated. The teachers realized their work was worth it.

Had Dana bailed out on her plan to implement a full inclusion model on emotional information alone, the students would have lost. Balancing information from technical data and emotional information is an art. There are times when emotional information may outweigh technical data. However, more times than not, principals fail to collect emotional data for fear of being accused of soliciting information and then not listening. Principals must collect all sorts of data, including emotional information. Even when hard data drives a final decision, the emotional information around that decision has immense impact on a principal's communication and implementation of the decision.

Reinforce the Importance of Feelings

Using emotional information does not mean school leaders must abandon logic or well-thought-out plans and make decisions based on their emotions or the emotions of others. It means that the more school leaders make decisions based on hard data, the greater the opportunity for staff members to develop the perceptions that you do not care about them or their input, only data. When making decisions, school leaders must do their best to listen, educate, and inform others. Never undervalue the emotions of others. Make decisions based on well-organized plans or lead collaborative groups in the decision-making progress.

After he made a decision that he thought was well-reasoned, a school leader became frustrated and angry when he heard that a teacher assigned to a duty as part of the "fallout" of his decision was upset. The school leader stated:

"Before learning about the value of emotional intelligence, I may have even sent an e-mail justifying why I moved the computers and that this was the way it was going to be. But instead, I went to the teacher. I asked her to explain how she felt. I explained to her I understood why she would feel this way, that I did not mean to hurt her feelings, and that I was sorry her feelings were hurt. I explained why I moved the computers and why I also had to assign a duty period. The fact that I took the time to seek her out, ask her how she felt, and express how I felt and why I chose to move the computers really made a difference."

Following up with staff members is cultivating the garden. Acknowledging the validity of her feelings helped the teacher move forward and accept the decision, helped heal the rift between principal and teacher, and cultivated cooperation in the computer lab instead of a potential "weed in the garden."

Reflection

1. What percentages of your decisions are made on technical data rather than emotional data? With which decisions are you more comfortable?

2. Think about the emotions of your staff the last time you made a decision based on hard data. Were they supportive of your decision? Did you care about your staff's emotions during the decision-making process?

3. When would you ever allow emotional information to outweigh the importance of technical or hard data in making a decision? When would you allow technical or hard data to outweigh the importance of emotional information in making a decision?

Steps to Improve your Emotional Reasoning

1. Ask others about their feelings about a decision you need to make. Ask them to differentiate between their gut feelings and what is really the best decision to make.

2. Explore your own feelings regarding a decision you have to make. Are you making the decision based on data or on emotions?

3. Make a list of decisions you make at work; beside the items on the list estimate how much emotional information and how much technical data go into the decisions.

CHAPTER 9
Self-Management

"We all have dreams. But in order to make dreams come into reality, it takes an awful lot of determination, dedication, self-discipline, and effort."

Jesse Owens

A rather obvious but under-recognized truth is that effectively managing one's own emotions can improve job satisfaction and enhance performance. The life of a school leader is filled with role conflicts and strains. The stress associated with this position, which requires long hours and results sometimes in little appreciation, has led to many state organizations predicting major shortages of principals in the near future. Despite a rise in salaries, emotional stress, including lack of appreciation and burnout, is contributing to the impending shortage. This chapter will give you some tools and strategies to increase your job satisfaction, reduce your stress, and improve your quality of life.

Managing your Emotions vs. Emotional Self-Control

Managing your emotions includes how you respond after tense emotional events or conflict and whether you can maintain a positive mood and continued effectiveness. Emotional self-control is the controlling of your own emotions at the time you perceive a threat. When principals learn how to manage their emotions, they increase their interpersonal effectiveness and quality of life. The school day does not usually end after one emotional situation, and even though you may have handled yourself well at the time, you must bring your "A game" the rest of the day. Further, when you go home after a tough day, your loved ones deserve a spouse, partner, or parent that can focus on the needs and pleasures of the family.

Many principals consider themselves effective in controlling their emotions during the time they are dealing with a person, group, or an intense event. However, *afterward*, their inability to manage their emotions creates adverse effects including poor encounters with another person or group, mood changes during the day, and lack of productivity for the remainder of the work day. Nearly every principal I have worked with individually or in groups has also admitted being short-tempered with someone in their personal lives because of an event that had happened many hours before at work. Learning to understand and manage emotions will have a positive effect on nearly every aspect of your life, and failure to manage emotions effectively can not only be detrimental to your quality of life but to your health as well. Numerous studies link chronic stress to aging, disease, and death.

The Snowball Effect of Unmanaged Emotions

Principals who have little understanding of their emotions and even less skill in managing them often feel unappreciated and get trapped in one emotional crisis after another. When dealing with a crisis or an intense situation at work, have you ever suddenly realized you have become withdrawn, moody, and short with other people? When principals do not take the time to sort out their thoughts or reflect on their emotions during an emotional event, they are often caught in an energy trap the remainder of the day.

Strategies for Managing your Emotions

There is no one best strategy, so think of each strategy you develop as a tool to be placed in your emotional intelligence toolbox. As you work on your development goals, practice these strategies. Eventually, you may find one or two "go to" strategies that you use most often when feeling emotionally challenged.

The power of positive intentions. Presuming positive intentions, one of the collaborative norms discussed earlier, is also an excellent strategy for managing and controlling your emotions. While this strategy is powerful for helping control one's emotions, it also happens to be my number one tool for managing my emotions.

Here are some examples of how it works. After an event or incident in which a person successfully controls his or her emotions, the person begins to reflect, or maybe even "cool down," even though throughout the whole incident, the person may not have shown any outward emotions. It is important to begin reflecting immediately after an event. Try to use the power of positive intentions in your reflection; try to honestly look at the event from another's point of view as if they had a positive purpose, a genuine question, or concern.

Each of the following incidents provoked a negative emotion and reaction from a principal who then shared the experience during a coaching session. Following each incident, the italics type shows how the principal could have used positive intentions to prevent the negative reaction.

1. An angry phone call or e-mail from a parent in the community: *The intention was that the parent wanted me to hear firsthand his frustration, and out of respect, he chose to contact me directly.*

2. A call from the superintendent inquiring about an event that happened in a building after you thought you had successfully handled it: *The superintendent must have received a call from the parent involved and just wants to touch base so he can honestly let the parent know that you had talked together about it.*

3. A meeting with a teacher and an official from the teachers' union: *The teacher really wanted to come to an agreement or consensus without writing a grievance.*

4. Without first talking with you, a meeting occurs between a teacher and the superintendent to discuss a concern about a situation in the building. *The teacher did not want to disappoint me or was afraid that she might get overly emotional if she talked to me first.*

These are just four examples of how presuming positive intentions can enable a principal to prevent emotions from causing them to behave ineffectively. Learning to manage your emotions contributes to overall life satisfaction.

Pausing. In the formula E + R = O (see also page 30), the important strategy is pausing and getting your head straight. What is the correct response that will most likely get the intended outcome? Although the value of pausing is commonly recognized, you would be surprised how many principals share with me that if they had just stopped and thought about how they were going to respond for a few seconds, they would have handled themselves differently.

Basically, pausing allows you to consider whether or not the amygdala has indeed sacrificed accuracy for speed. Is the event really a threat or life threatening? The key is to develop a habit that will enable you to exercise pausing. Some principals call it the five-second pause and during this time do a Stop-Look-Listen activity and try to figure out what emotions they are experiencing and why. To ensure I pause five seconds, especially when I am in larger groups, I bring one of my hands to my chin to suggest and demonstrate that I am in a "thinking mode." This really helps me in two areas. First, it allows me to pause, get my mind straight and Stop-Look-Listen, and second it allows me to really process what the other person is saying. If someone else is overly emotional, your pausing and listening rather than responding too quickly can defuse the situation helping both you and the other person.

What would you suggest to a colleague? One good tool is to remove yourself immediately from a situation and imagine it is happening to someone else, much like using a case study. Often if you remove yourself from an emotionally charged situation and the emotions associated with it, you would be able to give great advice to a colleague. Now what is important is to follow your own advice.

Question yourself and ask for proof. Where is the proof that this is truly happening? Has there ever been a situation like this before where you had some of the same feelings and beliefs and you were wrong? By asking yourself these two questions, you are assessing the accuracy of the perceived threat.

Probe for specificity. When you take time to pause and ask yourself questions about what you are thinking or feeling, you are truly probing for specificity. However, you can also use this as a strategy when someone else is emotionally hijacked. By probing for specificity you can help another person truly separate their thoughts from their emotions. A similar strategy is "Balancing Advocacy and Inquiry." When you really pause and take the time to probe into what people are feeling or thinking, you are well on your way to becoming an excellent principal. You can use some other strategies and ask, "Where is the truth?" or ask them if they are presuming positive intentions during this time. Many of the strategies in this book can be used to help your staff during conflict or emotional times.

Exercise, nutrition, rest. Exercise, nutrition, and rest have to be included in any list of strategies for controlling your emotions. Some administrators exercise before going home, and they have increased their health, well-being, and relationships at home. Others plan their days and practice reflection during morning workouts. Still others use reading, painting, playing video games, or doing needlepoint as a productive strategy for dealing with their emotion-filled days. Whatever the method, it is important to find one that works for you—and schedule time to do it.

Nutrition and rest are usually the first two areas sacrificed when principals move from their relaxed summers to their tense school years. Because of their busy schedules, many principals are challenged by maintaining proper nutrition. If you are nutritionally challenged, read a book detailing proper nutrition and diet's positive effect on your life. Keep a journal of what you are eating along with your emotional intelligence journal, and look for a relationship between your diet and your emotional ups and downs. Learning how to manage your emotions will help you rest and sleep better, and adequate rest and sleep will help you successfully manage your emotions.

Why Manage Your Emotions?

Simply to create a better you—one who will be more productive, have a greater influence on staff, be able to cultivate a committed culture, and improve your school as well as every other aspect of your personal and professional life. I tell people that when I was a middle school principal I had the very best job in the world. I got up every day and looked forward to going to school to be with adults as well as children. I could not always have said this, but after completing emotional intelligence training and practicing the skills involved, I became much more relaxed. People did not question my decisions because they did not like me; they questioned me because they needed more clarification. When parents called to ask questions, it was not because they did not trust me or the school; it is because they wanted to be involved.

There are many reasons for beginning today to develop and hone your emotional intelligence skills, if not for the sole reason that you want to enjoy your job more. Better health, better relationships, and less stress are just a few benefits of high emotional intelligence.

Emotional Intelligence at Home and School

Some administrators may think they can practice high emotional intelligence at school but not at home. Sam is principal of a junior high that produces excellent results in academics and athletics. Working 60–70 hours per week and visible at nearly every school function, Sam has the reputation for being fair, patient, understanding, and a very good listener. There may not be a better principal around. However, as a husband and father, Sam used to lack patience and understanding. In fact, Sam was a different person at work than at home. Allowing the role strain from a difficult job to affect his home and marriage, Sam managed his emotions poorly and lashed out at his wife and children. When Sam began developing his emotional intelligence, he wanted most to learn how to manage his emotions. By practicing reflection, presuming positive intentions, and using other strategies found here, Sam said he "felt like a new man."

Get Control of Your Life Today

To start living your life without stress and fear is impossible, but you can learn to live with less stress by managing your emotions. What is your first thought when

- The administrative assistant tells you a parent is on the phone for you?

- The superintendent stops by unexpectedly?

- You see an e-mail has arrived from a parent?

- You are called out of your office to a classroom?

- You walk into the office and a parent is waiting to see you?

Because we have all had the experiences above, we likely assign negative emotions to these events every time they happen—even before we know how they are going to turn out. However, with emotional intelligence training and an effort to reshape our pre-existing mental models, we can begin living and enjoying our lives and jobs again. When you open e-mails and try to find good and positive intentions in the text, you will be surprised at how positive they actually are. The same can be said with other aspects of your job. Now I am not suggesting being naïve and overly romantic about the world in which we live and work, but I encourage you to use the strategies in this chapter and start living a richer life today.

Reflection

1. Do you bring stress, frustration, and anger home? What does this look like?

2. Does any of the stress you experience at work take away from your happiness?

3. Describe the emotions that create your biggest challenges in being productive. Which emotions cause you the greatest stress?

Steps to Improve Your Emotional Self-Management

1. Try to identify your different emotions at work. Identify emotions that lead to negative feelings or negative moods. Identify emotions that lead to positive moods.

2. Understand that emotions usually drive thoughts and behavior. Think about some behaviors or feelings you would like to change. Identify the emotions associated with those behaviors and thoughts.

CHAPTER 10
Positive Influence

*"All this stuff doesn't happen to you for your own sake.
It doesn't happen to you so you can fill your shelves with
trophies or line your pockets with cash; it happens so you can
have a positive influence and encourage other people."*

David Robinson

Most people seeking improvement in emotional intelligence usually consider only the skill of managing their own emotions. However, leaders who can understand and manage the emotions of others have a powerful tool for leveraging extraordinary commitment and having a positive influence on their staff. And just like the other dimensions of emotional intelligence, you can develop and refine this skill.

In addition to generating greater performance from others, having a positive influence enables you to create a positive work environment and effectively deal with conflict in the workplace.

The inability to deal effectively with conflict is a common weakness of many school leaders. A popular joke is that the last class a school leader takes before becoming licensed is the class in which the spine is removed. Hypotheses abound about the reason for school leaders' difficulties in dealing with others' emotions, but I think it is usually caused by a lack of organizational awareness rather than a lack of concern for others' emotions. Intensely focused on whatever task is at hand, some principals fail to carve out time for dealing with emotions and sensitive issues. Leaders who are not aware of emotions and do not want to be aware of emotions are essentially isolated in a position of little organizational awareness.

Leading Your Staff to Greater Performance

Two basic human needs are (1) the need to be loved and (2) the need to know we are good enough. In Oprah Winfrey's Harvard commencement speech, she mentioned that she had conducted more than 3500 interviews over the years. She said that regardless of who she interviewed—past presidents, sitting presidents, rock stars, movie stars, famous athletes, addicts, convicts, artists—they all had one thing in common: the need for affirmation. When the interviews were over they always asked if it was good enough. She went on to add that even when she interviewed Beyonce in all her Beyonce-ness, when the camera and lights were turned off, she asked if the take was good enough. With this information, school leaders can connect with their staff by affirming their efforts and letting them know you care.

When leaders take the time to be sincerely aware of their staffs' emotions, teachers feel that their leaders care about them and will be loyal and committed.

Patience and Persistence

After completing her first year as principal, Elizabeth, a master at balancing patience and persistence, was ready to challenge her staff with implementing short cycle assessments, end-of-year assessments, additional interventions, and a new philosophy of relentlessly educating all children. Elizabeth's passion for excellence was refreshing for some but intimidating for others. Many of the faculty expressed concerns that she was overestimating their students' real potential, that their community did not highly value education, that not all students were ready to learn, and that many kids today were just different and impossible to reach.

After listening, Elizabeth affirmed her high confidence in the abilities of the faculty based on her year of watching them teach and build relationships with their students. Elizabeth stressed that the futures of their children depended on the level of learning that would take place within their school, and her hope was that every student would have the opportunity to be successful. Without a commitment to excellence and extra intervention for students, many of them would not have the opportunity for success. Elizabeth was appealing to her teachers' commitment to helping all children learn.

Some of the body language (dropping heads, slouching shoulders, rolling eyes) and some previous conversations with staff members told Elizabeth that there was fear in the room. Empathizing with her staff, she validated their fear and worries about the changes and then asked them to worry about the children's futures as well.

Unafraid of openly recognizing some common emotions that prevent change, Elizabeth instead focused on the hope of achievement to inspire and instill courage in her staff. Stressing that together they could develop a school that would not allow failure, she helped them envision a school in which every student could learn in an environment of mutual support and understanding.

Key to Elizabeth's message was her sincerity and authenticity. Quick to perceive insincerity, a faculty feeling manipulated by a "let's win one for the Gipper" speech will lose motivation. In fact, my experience working with leaders has shown that often the most verbal principals who speak with the most eloquence during speeches and pep talks are sometimes viewed by their staffs as manipulative. Elizabeth was giving more than a pep talk. She was emphasizing the great struggle that lay ahead, making it clear she would also face challenges caused by the changes. By assuring their staffs that they, too, will be challenged during the change process, principals can build enough support to launch reform initiatives.

While responding to the emotions of her staff, Elizabeth remained committed to sharing her vision of every student achieving success. A principal with a high level of emotional intelligence, Elizabeth managed the emotions of her staff by channeling their energy in a positive direction.

Creating a Positive Work Environment

Elizabeth had mastered one of the most important concepts in managing others' emotions. Although it was not prevalent during the meeting, much of Elizabeth's work had been done behind the scenes and informally. Whether it was during lunch, a conference time, or an after-school talk, Elizabeth probed for specificity about what emotions the staff was experiencing as she communicated the new vision. More important, Elizabeth delved deeper into the thinking of the staff that led to their emotions: "Why would you be angry if we started using more planning time for conferencing?" "What is the main source of the fear?" "Do you really think if you failed, you would lose your job?" By such probing, Elizabeth was able to discover some unproductive thought patterns that she could address and refute.

One was that the change would set teachers up for failure resulting in reprimands or even replacement. Elizabeth also learned that a decade earlier many of the staff had experienced their principal spending time, money, and resources to launch a somewhat similar initiative. When it failed due to lack of spending on professional development and implementation support, the teachers were blamed for a lack of commitment. Teachers remembered how this felt, for when emotions are evoked, people don't forget. Because she had worked to understand the reasons for the staff's hesitation, Elizabeth could dispel unfounded fears. After she felt well-versed on the thoughts and emotions of her staff, Elizabeth began to expand on communicating her vision and communicating hope and the emotions associated with the eventual successful attainment of the goals.

Jim Collins, in his book *Good to Great* (2001), stated that great companies did more with their "not to do" lists than their "to do" lists. Not only are "not to do" lists important for leading, but also, to go fast there are times you must go slowly. However, leadership is not always so simple, and sometimes in spite of negative emotions associated with a project or initiative, the leader must go on. Taking the time to understand the swirl of emotions allows the group to better prepare for obstacles that may occur later in the project. Just as important as listening to the emotions is identifying the underlying cause of the emotions, which usually takes the most time.

Dealing with Conflict

Emotionally intelligent leaders are great listeners. They understand that sometimes taking time to listen will complicate their already busy schedule, but showing people that you truly care by giving them the time they deserve pays off.

Sally has been a driven, task-oriented school leader for more than 10 years. She keeps a work pace rivaling a world championship thoroughbred on Derby Day in Lexington, Kentucky. While preparing for a presentation on student achievement for the board of education, she had closed her office door for about 15 minutes when Billy Smith's mother and father arrived at school wanting to discuss a disciplinary action taken with their son the previous day. His teasing and bullying of other students had earned him an after-school detention. Although Sally really felt rushed to finish the board presentation, she knew she needed to make time for the parents.

Opening her office door, Sally came out to meet Billy and his parents and invite them into her office to sit informally at a round table. Sally reminded herself not to assume the parents would protest the detention, not to defend the discipline of the school, and not to immediately discuss Billy's discipline record. Sally listened to Billy and probed for specific reasons why he felt he was having trouble interacting with his peers. Whenever the parents displayed anger at the school, Sally empathized by commenting that as a parent, she, too, would be very upset by the situation. Then, by reminding them that they were all on the same team, Sally would bring the parents back to the task at hand while directing the conversation toward finding solutions for Billy's behavior.

When the meeting finished almost an hour later, both parents thanked Sally for her time and left feeling satisfied with the outcome of the meeting. Billy still had his detention, and his parents knew the school was working with and not against them. Sally was glad that she had taken time to meet with the parents and that the meeting had been so productive, giving priority to her main responsibility of serving students and parents.

Balancing Advocacy and Inquiry

Although Sally has the verbal and analytical skills to win nearly every debate she enters, and her ability to influence has labeled her as someone that could sell "snow to Eskimos," she realized that most people just want the opportunity to be heard. In her early years, she would dominate the conversations and always had the last word. Sally began to notice that after several interactions with her, people would not come to her as often and started choosing her assistants as listeners.

Now, along with being a great listener, Sally has committed to the process of balancing advocacy and inquiry. Instead of solely advocating her ideas or suggestions, Sally takes the time to really hear and understand the ideas and suggestions of others. After everyone has had an opportunity to share, she usually concludes by saying "let's discuss what we think is the best idea or combine the suggestions to make a new idea." This conclusion reminds her and everyone else that she is not trying to get everyone to agree to her idea but to come up with the best decision.

Parents, teachers, and students now like to communicate with Sally. The keys to balancing advocacy and inquiry are to (1) Pause, (2) Listen, (3) Be aware of your and others' emotions, (4) Listen—avoid solving problems or giving advice immediately, (5) Paraphrase and ask for clarification, and (6) Resolve the problem together. Meetings can become much more productive when shareholders really try to understand where other team members are coming from, thus the inquiry.

Very few school leaders lack the confidence, verbal skills, or the ability to influence. However, time and time again we hear that school leaders are not good listeners. Of course in reality, school leaders are listening—at least some of the time. But recall from earlier in the book that decision making is improved when you balance technical data and emotional information. Once you make a decision that's not in agreement with someone else's position, they can and will sometimes assert, "You didn't listen!" However, the more times you do take the time to listen and acknowledge others' feelings, most people will be able to understand your reasoning and follow your lead even if you make an unpopular decision.

Reflection

1. Can you describe a time when you successfully managed the emotions of others? What did you do that was so successful? How did your staff respond? What were your emotions at the time?

2. Can you describe a time when you did not successfully manage the emotions of others? What did you do that limited your success to manage the emotions of others? Describe your emotions at the time.

3. Have you ever witnessed a mentor who was great at managing the emotions of others? What did they do differently from those who do not manage the emotions of others well? What skills do they have?

Steps to Improve Your Positive Influence

1. Keep an emotional journal. Write down your work experiences of dealing with others during emotional times.

2. Observe others' emotions. Observe how people deal with those who are emotional. Make mental notes or notes in a journal about your observations.

3. Identify the actions or experiences that make you feel good at work. Practice applying these to others in the workplace.

4. Practice becoming a better active listener. Suspend your beliefs and paraphrase when possible.

CHAPTER 11
Summary

"The key to successful leadership today is influence, not authority."

Ken Blanchard

There is never a shortage of great educational research of specific practices and strategies that have a significant influence on school culture and accelerating student learning. Some of this research has been shared in this book. We know that a valued and engaged staff that focuses on student learning will have a significant impact on student learning. However, some school leaders do not regularly model the behaviors and practices associated with increasing the engagement level of their staff.

While I was writing this book, researcher John Hattie had been sharing new research from his meta-analyses on more than 800 studies on education practices. Hattie now reports that Collective Teacher Efficacy (CTE) has the greatest impact on student learning (1.57 effect size). This effect is double the effect of student feedback (.75 effect size). What many educators do not know is that collective efficacy research is more than two decades old, and it is only now through Hattie's meta-analyses of school research, that many practitioners are hearing about it for the first time. Many educators are asking, "What is Collective Teacher Efficacy, and how do we develop it?"

Collective Teacher Efficacy is the perception of teachers in a school that the faculty, as a whole, can have a positive impact and influence on student learning. CTE is more powerful than Teacher Self Efficacy and is greater than the sum of an entire staff having high levels of self-efficacy. The purpose of sharing this is that two of three strategies for developing greater CTE are closely related to emotional intelligence and the culture of the school. Collective Teacher Efficacy can only be increased in the school when there is trust in the school leader and a culture of purposeful teacher collaboration has been established. Only leaders with high levels of emotional intelligence can lead a culture of trust and collaboration. The third strategy is helping the school leader be viewed as an instructional/learning leader.

In closing, there are no great schools without great leadership. Great school leaders know how to model the behaviors and practices that align with the school's beliefs and values. Modeling emotional intelligence and having the right mindset are key for any school leader wanting to have a positive influence on school culture and a significant impact on student learning.

References

Achor, S. (2010). *The happiness advantage: The seven principals of positive psychology that fuel success and performance at work.* New York: Broadway.

Achor, S. (2011). The happy secret to better work [video]. Retrieved from https://www.ted.com/talks/shawn_achor_the_happy_secret_to_better_work

Ashton, P. T., & Webb, R. B. (1986). *Making a difference: Teachers' sense of efficacy and student achievement.* White Plains, NY: Longman.

Barling, J., Slater, F., & Kelloway, E. K. (2000). Transformational leadership and emotional intelligence: An exploratory study. *Leadership & Organization Development Journal, 21*(3), 157–161.

Battelle for Kids. (2015). *Five strategies for creating a high-growth school.* Retrieved from http://www.battelleforkids.org/docs/default-source/publications/soar_five_strategies_for_creating_a_high-growth_school.pdf?sfvrsn=2

Buckingham, M. (1999). *First, break all the rules: What the world's greatest managers do differently.* New York: Simon and Schuster.

Collins, J. (2001). *Good to great.* New York: HarperCollins.

DuFour, R. & Burnette, B. (2002). Pull out negativity by its roots. *Journal of Staff Development, 23*(3), 27-30.

DuFour, R., & Eaker, R. (1998). *Professional learning communities at work: Best practices for enhancing student achievement.* Bloomington, IN: National Educational Service.

Fullan, M. (2001). *Leading in a culture of change.* San Francisco: Jossey-Bass.

Garmston, R., & Wellman, B. (2009). *The adaptive school. A sourcebook for developing collaborative groups.* Norwood, MA: Christopher-Gordon.

Genos Emotional Intelligence Accreditation Manual. (2005). Swinburne University, Australia: Genos Pty Ltd.

George, J. M. (2000). Emotions and leadership: The role of emotional leadership. *Human Relations, 53*(8), 1027–1055.

Goleman, D. (1995). *Emotional intelligence.* New York: Bantam Books.

Heifetz, R. A., & Linsky, M. (2002). *Leadership on the line: Staying alive through the dangers of leading.* Boston: Harvard Business School Press.

Law, K. S., Song, L. J., & Wong, C. S. (2004). The construct and criterion validity of emotional intelligence and its potential utility for management studies. *Journal of Applied Psychology, 89*(3), 483–496.

Moore, B. L. (2007, September). *The emotional intelligence coaching of school administrators: A comparative case study.* Paper presented at the First International Congress on Emotional Intelligence, Malaga, Spain.

Palmer, B. (2003). *An analysis of the relationships between various models and measures of emotional intelligence.* Unpublished doctoral dissertation. Swinburne University, Victoria, Australia.

Pink, Daniel. (2009). *Drive: The surprising truth about what motivates us.* New York: Riverhead.

Reeves, D. (2002). *The leader's guide to standards: A blueprint for educational equity and excellence.* San Francisco: Jossey-Bass.

Sala, F. (2001). *Do programs designed to increase emotional intelligence at work-work?* Unpublished report of The Hay Group, Boston.

Salovey, P., & Mayer, J. D. (1990). Emotional intelligence. *Imagination, Cognition and Personality, 9*(3), 185–211.

Senge, P. M. (1990). *The fifth discipline. The art and practice of the learning organization.* New York: Doubleday.

Stone, H., Parker, J. D., & Wood, L. M. (2005). *Report on the Ontario Principals' Council leadership study.* Retrieved from http://www.eiconsortium.org/

About the Author

Dr. Bobby Moore began his career in the classroom, teaching at the middle school, high school, and post-secondary levels. Moore is also a former principal, superintendent, and senior director for the national not-for profit organization Battelle for Kids (BFK). His career in education and his work at BFK have been dedicated to inspiring and motivating educators through collaboration, professional development, innovation, and a laser-like focus on ensuring that all students reach their fullest potential. Dr. Moore's ability to provide thought leadership, strategize, build relationships, develop talent, and deliver high quality professional learning has allowed him the opportunity to experience much success as a school leader. In 2007, he was one of only four secondary principals originally selected to serve on the Governor's Institute on Creativity and Innovation in Education to help generate ideas for reforming education in Ohio. During his tenure as principal, Canaan Middle School received both state and national recognition for outstanding student achievement, value-added growth, and meeting the emotional and social needs of students. After leaving Canaan Middle School to be a superintendent in another district, Dr. Moore was able to apply what he refers to as "the same middle school support structures" he implemented at Canaan Middle School throughout an entire district. In just two years, the district received the highest rating for achievement in the state, including the honor of "Distinction," and ranked among the best in student growth data among all districts in Ohio.

During his tenure at Battelle for Kids, Dr. Moore led one of the largest school improvement collaboratives in the United States, was team lead on a statewide leadership academy for the Kentucky Department of Education, served as project lead for a statewide collaborative in Texas for elementary principals, and delivered workshops and keynotes for state departments of education, state associations, and national associations all over the country. While at Battelle for Kids, Dr. Moore had the opportunity to observe best practices, build relationships, and create networks with educators throughout the world. Some of the experiences and lessons learned are included in this book.

After approximately 25 years in education and six years at Battelle for Kids, Dr. Moore is the founder, president, and CEO of the EPIC Impact Education Group. EPIC Impact Education Group was founded to provide strategic counsel and partner with national and state organizations, education associations, and businesses, as well as urban, rural, suburban, and community schools to leverage strengths, accelerate growth, and increase efficiencies for maximum impact. Dr. Moore is a keynote speaker and author of several published professional journals and the book *Inspire, Motivate, Collaborate*. When not helping schools across the country or speaking at conferences, you may find Bobby traveling the world skiing, biking, or hiking. You can follow Bobby on twitter @DrBobbyMoore for relevant blogs and to follow the adventures of his famous dog, Bode.

CPSIA information can be obtained
at www.ICGtesting.com
Printed in the USA
FFHW01n1551050818
47653442-51262FF

9 781560 902959